ONE *second* AT A TIME

ONE *second*
AT A TIME

MY STORY
OF PAIN AND RECLAMATION

DIANE MORRISSEAU,
with ELISABETH BRANNIGAN

Foreword by Marlyn Bennett

PURICH
BOOKS

Printed in Canada on FSC-certified ancient-forest-free paper
(100% post-consumer recycled) that is processed chlorine- and acid-free.

UBC Press is a Benetech Global Certified Accessible™ publisher.
The epub version of this book meets stringent accessibility standards,
ensuring it is available to people with diverse needs.

LIBRARY AND ARCHIVES CANADA CATALOGUING IN PUBLICATION

Title: One second at a time : my story of pain and reclamation /
Diane Morrisseau, with Elisabeth Brannigan ; foreword by Marlyn Bennett.

Names: Morrisseau, Diane, author. | Brannigan, Elisabeth, author.

Identifiers: Canadiana (print) 20230620191 | Canadiana (ebook) 20230620299 |
ISBN 9780774880978 (softcover) | ISBN 9780774880992 (EPUB) |
ISBN 9780774880985 (PDF)

Subjects: LCSH: Morrisseau, Diane. | LCSH: Abused wives—Canada—
Biography. | LCSH: Victims of family violence—Canada—Biography. |
LCSH: Family violence—Canada. | LCSH: Women—Abuse of—Canada. |
LCSH: Women—Violence against—Canada. | LCGFT: Autobiographies.

Classification: LCC HV6626.23.C3 M67 2024 | DDC 362.82/92092—dc23

Canada Council   Conseil des arts
for the Arts   du Canada

Canadä

BRITISH COLUMBIA
ARTS COUNCIL

BRITISH
COLUMBIA

UBC Press gratefully acknowledges the financial support for our publishing
program of the Government of Canada, the Canada Council for the Arts,
and the British Columbia Arts Council.

*UBC Press is situated on the traditional, ancestral,
and unceded territory of the xʷməθkʷəy̓əm (Musqueam) people.
This land has always been a place of learning for the xʷməθkʷəy̓əm,
who have passed on their culture, history, and traditions for millennia,
from one generation to the next.*

Purich Books, an imprint of UBC Press
University of British Columbia
Vancouver, BC
www.purichbooks.ca

For those women and children
who are out there suffering like I once did.
You are not alone and there is hope for you.
And most especially for my children:
Errol, Donna, Sharon, Karen, and Randy.

– DIANE MORRISSEAU

For my children:
Kenzie, Christian, Ogimaa Kwe, and Tecumseh.

– ELISABETH BRANNIGAN

CONTENTS

FOREWORD

A Tapestry of Truths

THROUGHOUT THE ANNALS of history, stories have been the thread that binds humanity; weaving cultures, eras, and civilizations together. In this intricate mosaic certain stories shimmer with a distinct luminance, their narratives echoing louder and longer than others, touching souls across epochs. They tell tales of unwavering courage, the ability to overcome unimaginable adversities, and a resilience that challenges the very fabric of human fragility. The journey you're about to delve into, that of an eighty-one-year-old Indigenous woman, epitomizes this luminosity. This narrative is not merely woven tales; it's a profound tapestry of truths. Diane Morrisseau's life unveils a raw and riveting account of one Indigenous woman's fierce battle for safety in a world that often diminished her worth. Opportunities for her to find security were few and far between as she grappled with the violence of her husband, an Indigenous man who should have been her protector and the loving father of her children. Tragically, burdened by the profound weight of colonization, he mirrored the very violence that was likely inflicted upon him. Diane's story is more than just a chronicle of years lived, it's a powerful testament to the depths of human endurance, to her own indomitable spirit and resilience, and to her quest for freedom, dignity, and self-realization in the face of even the darkest adversities. Through the experiences she shares, we witness the raw power of maternal love and its uncanny ability to fuel resistance against the most oppressive forces. It reminds us that the spirit, once ignited with the flame of determination and hope, can combat the most torrential storms of life.

Domestic violence, a grim shadow that looms over countless households, has unfortunately established itself as a pervasive issue across cultures and societies. Yet, the anguish and torment captured in these pages surpass typical understanding and delve into an abyss of cruelty and pain that is truly gut-wrenching. Diane Morrisseau, ensnared in a life rife with betrayal, escalating violence, and a deep-seated disdain, paints a bleak yet poignant portrait that many Indigenous women may tragically recognize. Every harrowing episode, tear shed, and silent scream echoes the shared trauma of countless souls. This narrative, while deeply personal, serves as a stark mirror that reflects the deeply entrenched systemic issues that have persistently plagued and oppressed Indigenous communities since contact with settler societies. It highlights the intricate interplay between personal suffering and collective historical trauma, underscoring the pressing need for awareness, understanding, and reform – as vital today as it was during the distressing times recounted by the author.

While I have never met Diane personally, her narrative is reminiscent of stories I've heard from numerous Indigenous women and resonates deeply with my own harrowing experiences. In my past I faced the chilling grasp of domestic violence and was immersed in a tumultuous sea of emotions and obstacles. The fear-laden nights, days shrouded in shame, and those silent, desperate pleas for help are paths I've also unfortunately traversed. These experiences, while intensely personal, are threads of pain shared by many Indigenous women. Our individual traumas are amplified by the burdens of our collective scars: remnants of historical and societal injustices that persistently plague our communities.

Yet, amid this despair, I found solace in the transformative power of "re-storying," which is reflected in the way that Diane shares her lived experience with interpersonal violence. It's a deeply cathartic journey where one revisits, comprehends, and then narrates their personal experiences, effectively rewriting the narrative from one of pain to one of empowerment. This process is not merely therapeutic, it provides a sense of agency, giving a voice to those silenced by oppression and offering an authentic platform to speak one's truth.

When Diane meticulously transcribes her experiences, she offers us more than a mere memoir – she invites us into the sacred space of her Debwewin journey. Rooted in Anishinabe wisdom, the Debwewin journey represents a profound alignment of the mind and heart, culminating in a deeply personal revelation of truth. It's a transformative exploration where introspection and experience meld, crafting a narrative that is both uniquely individual and universally resonant. Through her narrative, Diane not only uncovers her own innermost truths but also illuminates a path for others. Her words become both a testimony of resilience and a beacon that encourages others to embark on their own Debwewin journeys, to seek enlightenment, truth, and ultimate liberation.

In an era where the haunting spectre of missing and murdered Indigenous women is a grim reality, stories like these are not just poignant reminders but essential accounts that demand attention. Each one unveils the layers of systemic violence and cultural obliteration imprinted upon

Indigenous communities and borne out of the legacy of
colonialism. They delve deep into the traumatic after-effects
on Indigenous men, who, having endured the oppressive
colonial structures of residential schools, manifest their
suffering in heart-wrenching ways, sometimes culminating
in violence against those they love. They also underscore
the unwavering strength of Indigenous women – their
determination to rise above adversity, and their relentless
pursuit of justice and truth. They are heartrending
alarms, sirens calling out for urgent recognition.

To the courageous woman, Diane, who bears her soul
in these pages:

> Your legacy is immortalized in your words. Your testament,
> rich in depth and truth, stands as a luminous beacon,
> guiding not just women, both Indigenous and beyond,
> but humanity at large. It lights a way, drawing individuals
> from the bleak shadows of anguish and brutality,
> ushering them toward hope and healing. The tenacity
> you've shown, the ceaseless love you've held for your
> children even in the face of unspeakable odds, and
> your transformative journey from vulnerability to
> empowerment are a resounding affirmation of the
> indomitable spirit of human endurance, spirit, and
> resilience. Your story is both a testament to personal
> strength and a call to collective understanding.

To the reader:

> As you immerse yourself in the words and experiences
> chronicled within this book, it's essential to grasp that
> it extends beyond the boundaries of a personal memoir.
> This narrative stands as a fervent call to action, an
> impassioned plea for compassion and empathy, and

a formidable rallying cry that seeks to instigate transformation. It serves as a bridge, seeking to connect human souls through shared understanding and collective responsibility. It is my hope that in sharing Diane's story, we inch closer to a world where no woman has to ever endure the pain and anguish that Diane details in these pages.

Let *One Second at a Time* stand as a monumental testament to the boundless fortitude of Indigenous women like Diane Morrisseau, who have weathered centuries of adversity yet remain undeterred in spirit and unbroken in resolve. And let it inspire hope – a hope for a brighter horizon where her tale is not just told but celebrated, and where her truth is not just acknowledged but revered and protected, so it reverberates for generations to come.

– MARLYN BENNETT

PREFACE

THE IDEA TO WRITE my story began a long time ago, shortly
after I left my husband Edgar. I made that break in 1979.
So many terrible things have happened to me in my life.
I've learned a lot of life's lessons. That's how I see it now,
but there was a time I was in such a black place that I
thought I was never going to get out. I was suicidal. There
was no hope, but I survived. I don't feel sorry for myself.
It was quite a journey, my journey.

When I started going to Al-Anon, I began talking about
my life and the things that were happening to me. I heard
other women's stories and could relate to them, and it was
there that I met Bernelda Wheeler, who was the first to
encourage me to write my story. She said my story could
help others, and I knew she was right. She was an author
and offered to help me turn my story into a book. Sadly, she
passed away before I was ready to see the project through,
but she remains an inspiration in my mind and heart as I
work towards fulfilling my dream of sharing my story with
the world.

I started writing back in 1980. For about three years I
would write in this big, thick scribbler. I had lots in there, but
my husband Edgar was behind these break-ins I was having

at my house. One day my scribbler was gone. He had them take it. I felt discouraged and I stopped for a while. I tried to start again because I was going to give it to Bernelda to start writing my book. But it was just so overwhelming, and I kept thinking I wasn't meant to write it. I remember that.

But people kept telling me that my story gave them hope. I was talking about my story with a woman I knew around that time, and she told me, "Diane, you must write it. It will give hope to a lot of people. It sure gave me hope." She would connect me with women to talk with and listen to. They would share what they were going through, and I found that I could really help them by sharing my experiences with them. That's how I started working in a shelter as a counsellor. I could relate and I wanted to help them. Even at my age, and even though I'm technically retired, I still do counselling at the Treatment Centre in Sagkeeng and in a women's shelter too. I just know when a woman needs to talk to someone. I do counselling with them and try to give them hope. I give them resources and share ideas, but one thing I never do is give advice. I will never tell them to leave because that just doesn't work.

I also knew I wanted to tell my story for my kids. I wasn't a good mother. I never was, and I want them to understand why. One reason was that I never learned parenting skills. I was very young when I had my kids. I didn't show them any affection. I didn't tell my kids I loved them or praise them. I never got that, and I didn't know that it was important. I didn't do any of the things you're supposed to do raising a child. I didn't focus on them; I was focusing on their dad. All my time and energy went into trying to please him because I was so scared. I just didn't know how to be a mother.

They're all troubled. None of them finished high school and now they struggle financially. They couldn't learn in school because of all the trauma they experienced. Three of

them for sure were diagnosed with post-traumatic stress
disorder and mental health issues. They have addictions –
some severe. We were always walking on eggshells, and
my kids felt it. They were beaten and put down every day.
I didn't know that then. I didn't know how bad the abuse
was for them too. He was abusive to all of us. I was no help.
I didn't know any better. I can see that the way they are
today, all their struggles stem from their childhood. I see
all the damage that was done. They have issues with me,
especially my daughters. I see this with a lot of young
mothers who I work with, and this is very common. The
young girls have issues with their mothers. Because of
our own trauma we're not good mothers.

I want to let my kids know, too, that I'm not doing any of
this out of hate. They just need to know the truth. Everything!
It's always good for the truth to come out. I want my kids to
recognize why I made the mistakes that I did. That I didn't
know any better. I want them to see me, the changes that
I've made in my life and the way I am today. I want them to
see the past clearly and know that they can also move past
all that pain and do well for themselves. They can do it and
have a good life for themselves too.

Bernelda wanted to help me write my story. Even years
later, when she was getting sick with cancer and couldn't do
the writing for me, she said she would give me a name of
another author who could work with me. So I was given this
guy's name, and we met up with him. But then he was moving
to Vancouver or something, so he gave me the name of
another writer. This guy was a Jehovah's Witness. He started
helping me to write my book. I was meeting him once a
week, but he couldn't handle it. He'd stop me from talking.
His face would just go red, and he would say, "I can't do it
anymore. We need to stop." So I got discouraged there again
for a while. I thought it was not meant to be, I guess. But

I always had that feeling that I needed to do it. Something
told me not to give up. Working with women especially,
I felt that. I have a really strong desire to help people
because of what I went through.

I still wanted to tell my story. I wanted to find someone
to help me. Then in 2011, I met Elisabeth Brannigan at the
Mino Pimatiziwin Family Treatment Centre in Sagkeeng.
I was the cultural helper and counsellor there, and she was
the teacher. I'm trying to remember how it happened and
what I said. I don't know, but I remember the feeling that
I needed to find someone to help me finish the book. I told
her about my dream of having my story published, and she
offered to help. I forget exactly what I said to her, but it
started to happen. My dream was finally coming to life.

Elisabeth's husband Jerry Fontaine is my cousin and was
a good friend of my sister Juliana. She used to work with
him when he was chief. I didn't know him well back then,
but I always heard good things about him. He was very
supportive to the people in our community and helped me
when no one else would.

Jerry conducted a pipe ceremony to start us off in a good
way. We would smudge before our talks and whenever
things got hard. It wasn't easy. When we started, I would
go and see Elisabeth all the time. I remember the feeling I
would get as I was going down the road to her place. I was
already feeling the pain. I was thinking about all the things
we were going to talk about – there were so many things.

I wasn't sure where to begin. Throughout the process
I wondered whether I should talk about my whole life, or
just my life with Edgar. I often wonder which was harder.
The thing is, I know in the book I talk more about my
relationship with Edgar. It's not that he is more important,
but it is, at least in part, because I remember more. Because
of the trauma I suffered as a child, with the sexual abuse and

all that stuff in the school, I don't remember everything. It's like a dream in some parts, coming to me in flashbacks, and then I don't know what happened exactly. I blocked out so much. I included everything I could though, because I know that the things that happened to me as a child, good and bad, helped shape me into the person I was, and the person I am today.

So Elisabeth and I would meet, and I would tell my story. She recorded me and sometimes asked questions. I would talk and sometimes cry. It was very draining, and it would take some time to recuperate from these talks. Sometimes I kind of dreaded going to her place, because I knew how hard it would be. Sometimes I felt that I couldn't go on anymore. I just couldn't. That's why I did a lot of self-care. I continue to do this self-healing work. I've Sundanced, and I continue to go to ceremonies along with other therapy work. I see a psychologist. And I once asked him, "Why do I still cry when I've done all this work?" He answered, "Because the memory will always be there." I'm over eighty and I still cry!

This book is so important to me, and I'm happy it's finally going to happen. I got discouraged many times during this whole process, thinking it was never going to happen, and I would put it out of my head for a while. I was giving up, thinking my story wasn't meant to be. That's what I was thinking. But Elisabeth kept writing, and she and Jerry kept encouraging me to have hope. They would always keep me informed, letting me know how things were going.

There was one time a publisher was interested. The editor changed her mind right before we were to sign a contract. I'm not sure why she changed her mind at the last minute. This was tough because it was exciting to think it was going to be published, and then everything just fell through. Again, I figured it was not meant to be.

But now here we are. My dream is really coming true. I'm not well, and going over my story again is hard. It's taking a lot out of me. I feel drained. I'm older now and I'm more sensitive. I get tired more easily and sometimes I'm too sick to work. But I'm hopeful now that I will live to see my book published to help people. That is ultimately what this is all about. I am truly grateful for the life I have lived because it has given me the strength and wisdom to fulfill my life's purpose. I have dedicated myself to using the wisdom I have gained through my experiences to helping others, and I believe this book could really make a difference. I am told again and again that sharing my story is a powerful tool and that I have knowledge and experience that is valuable. I am appreciated. I am seen as strong and wise. I am in a place in my life where I can finally accept this, where I know that it's true, and I am proud of the woman I have become. I feel good about myself. I feel good about my life.

This book is for my kids and all the women who might feel trapped and without hope. I think if they read my book and see the changes that I made in my life, they will see that there is always hope.

PROLOGUE

I WAS A CHILD when we met. He began grooming me almost immediately, but most of the work was already done for him. The abandonment and abuse I suffered as a child left me vulnerable to monsters like him. I was with Edgar for eighteen years. The last ten years were hell because he controlled me in every way. I tried to leave so many times, but he would always find me. He would threaten to kill my kids and tell me that if I wanted to see them grow up, I had to do what he wanted. These were not empty or idle threats. He was a psychopath. I was married to a murderer. That's one of the reasons why I didn't leave: I knew I would always be looking over my shoulder if I did. That's what stopped me for eighteen years. That's why I stayed so long.

I used to have a lot of pictures from my childhood. Now I don't have any pictures of me when I was a child. Edgar burned all of them because he was jealous of my pictures, jealous of any life I had without him. He burned my pictures, destroying any image of who I was before I met him. In the eighteen years I was with him, it was like I had been fed to the flames just like my pictures. I was completely consumed, rendered unrecognizable, and seemingly destroyed by him. But I got out. The burns were so deep I wanted to die; I have

so many scars that I look like a different person. I was left
with a pain that I will carry for the rest of my life, yet I
survived. I walked out of the hell that was my life with
Edgar. I was lost for a long time, and the image of who
I was changed forever, but I remain, and I am thriving.

A NOTE ON THE TEXT

ALL THE STORIES in this book are true. Others may remember things differently, but the events described within are portrayed to the best of Diane Morrisseau's memory. Some names and identifying details have been changed to protect the privacy of the people involved.

This book contains content that some may find disturbing. Readers who have experienced similar trauma are encouraged to have a self-care plan in place, to remember their strengths, and to seek help if needed.

ONE *second* AT A TIME

1

A Perfect Home

FOR THE LONGEST TIME I thought it was normal not to
remember anything before eight or nine years old. When I
heard my friends talk about things that happened when they
were young, I thought they were lying. When I began my
healing journey, I had to look back to understand my life
and all that has happened to me. Initially, I had to learn
about my early childhood from what people told me. For
the longest time I had no memories of my own. Then one
day, I began to have flashbacks. Memories from those early
years flooded into my consciousness, vivid but incomplete.
Looking back was like trying to piece together a series of
dreams and nightmares. Making sense of these foggy
glimpses into the early events of my life has helped me to
understand why things happened the way they did. Facing
the realities of my childhood is still painful, but seeking the
truth led me to a place where I could learn to forgive those
who hurt me, and to forgive myself.

I was born in 1943 on Sagkeeng First Nation, an Ojibway-
Anishinabe community situated where the Winnipeg River
empties into Lake Winnipeg. My biological parents were
J.B. Morrisseau and Annie Gerard. I have six biological
siblings – five sisters and one brother; Joanne being the

oldest, followed by Martha, Helena, Rita, and Caroline, then Joseph, Juliana, and myself being the youngest.

When I was a baby, we lived in Victoria Beach where my biological dad was working at the time. I never really knew him because he left when I was still a baby. Most of what I know about my parents came from my Auntie Agnes. She was my mother's sister, and I became very close to her. She's gone now too. From what my Auntie Agnes told me, my dad was a hard worker and good provider. I used to go hide at her place sometimes when I would run away from my husband, Edgar. After seeing my bruises and black eyes, she would often tell me, "That's one thing your dad never did." She'd add, "Your mom never had marks on her face or black eyes. Yeah, he was a womanizer, but he was a good provider and he never laid a hand on your mom."

My Auntie Agnes also shared a few stories about my mother, who was very pretty, fair with a few little freckles. She told me once, "You're so much like your mom. You know, she liked to sew clothes. She sewed her own dresses and clothes for her children, just like you do now." I guess I was like her all right, because I sewed a lot when my kids were small. I made blankets when I could get old winter coats. I would take them apart, cut them in squares, and sew them together. I used to like hearing these stories about my mother. I was also told that she liked to laugh, and that she liked dancing to music on the radio. That was another thing I had in common with her.

I was in my forties when I learned about what happened to my mother. I don't know if I want to talk about those things, about how she died. It's odd, but when I found out that my dad had cheated on my mother, I didn't really have an issue with it. I felt it was their business. I was less forgiving of my mother. She was hurt and very angry because my dad was cheating on her. My dad gave her a sexually transmitted infection over and over again. Finally, it got to the point where she didn't want to get better. She just let it kill her. The sickness killed her because she refused to go to the hospital. She just wanted to die. I think she could have gotten better if she had wanted to. Initially I thought, "What a selfish woman. She just thought of herself. She left me here to suffer all over the place. You might as well say she killed herself." I suffered without her, and it took me a long time to forgive her once I knew the truth.

For the longest time I felt abandoned and betrayed by my mother for choosing to give up. Eventually I realized that she was suffering, and I understood her desperation. I saw myself in her. My mother experienced a lot of the same things that I experienced. It is incredible how history seems to repeat itself, sometimes in the strangest of ways. Not only did my husband cheat on me, too, he actually fooled around with the daughters of these women who had affairs with my dad. So I had to face what happened to my mother to deal with the things that happened to me too. Finding forgiveness for my mother helped me heal and forgive myself and those people who hurt us both. I can't carry that stuff.

I was only six months old when my mother died. My dad sent us away the same day she died, and then went out west alone. When they took us, I was on the bed with some of my siblings who were all playing, jumping, and laughing. My oldest sister, Joanne, who must have been about twelve at this time, was looking after us. It was my father's uncle, John Morrisseau, and his wife, Clara, who brought all of us kids downstairs. Juliana talked about seeing our sister Rita being taken away and being put into a boat and crossing the river with a family. She talked about feeling sad and wanting to go with her.

We were separated. Some of us were placed with family or in foster homes while the older ones were sent to residential

school. I was in a few different foster homes in the months
following my mother's death. I've learned since then that
they weren't very good homes. It was good that I was
adopted before too long. I was the only one of my siblings
who ever really had a home. None of them were adopted;
they were all just kind of sent from place to place.

Since I was too young to remember when my siblings and
I were taken, I didn't even know about them for the longest
time. It was not until I was around ten years old when my
sister Juliana and brother Joseph came to live with us that
I learned the truth. Before then, Juliana and Joseph went
to residential school, and I think they stayed at our Auntie
Esther's when they weren't in school. It would have been
in the early 1950s that they began staying with us during
their holidays. It was kind of strange when they first came.
Nobody prepared me, and I had no idea that they were my
sister and brother. No one even ever told me I was adopted
or that I had biological siblings. I don't even know how I
found out they were my sister and brother when they came
for the first time. It was like they suddenly appeared and
were just there, a part of the family we'd never talked about.

There was only a two-year age difference between Juliana
and me. We got along really well. Every summer they would
come to stay with us, and Juliana and I became very close as
we got older. We talked about everything. We used to do a
lot of stupid things together, and we laughed all the time.
We used to like laughing, and I remember I made her laugh
a lot. She'd even have tears in her eyes because she'd be
laughing so much. We were good friends.

Joseph, on the other hand, was quiet. He was given chores
to do, which he did without complaint, and he was always
helpful around the house. But Joseph didn't like me. I didn't
get along with him and I was scared of him. As we got older,
things got very complicated. His actions had a profound

impact on my body image and self-esteem. He left when I was about thirteen and I never saw him again.

I never really had a relationship with my oldest sister Joanne, and we were never all that close. She was much older than me and wasn't around much. Maybe that's why we were never close. I wasn't close to my sister Helena when we were kids either, but we met as young adults and got along. I would stay with her sometimes as we got older. Helena was called Weegwas (which means "birch bark" in Ojibway) because she was so fair.

My other sister Rita lived with the Spences growing up. It was Maria Spence that brought her up. They lived in Powerview, a white community near the reserve. I think the Spences kept my sister Joanne also. She was twelve and in residential school though, so she wouldn't have been there much. When she turned sixteen, she got married and left school. She didn't stay with that guy too long because he drank a lot and wasn't very nice to her. She remarried a white guy from Lac du Bonnet who treated her better. They had two sons and a daughter. My sister Juliana and I used to go visit them once in a while.

I was about eight years old or so when I last saw Caroline. She came to stay with us for a little while during the summer holidays that year. It was just for that one summer though, and then I never saw her again after that. Apparently when she turned sixteen years old, she left school and hitchhiked to Vancouver to find our dad. That's how my sister Caroline ended up out there, and she never came back.

I think she died in 1967. She would have been thirty-two years of age. It's a sad story. I just met her kids recently. Her daughter found me. We'd been looking for each other for over thirty-seven years. I thought they were in Hong Kong. When my sister died, their father, who was Chinese, told my dad that he was going to take them there. So for years that's

where I thought they were, but all this time they were in
Vancouver! We just found each other about ten years ago.
I went to Vancouver to meet them. My niece has four children
– two sons and two daughters. It meant a lot to me to connect
with them. My sister Juliana also moved to Vancouver and
lived with Caroline for a couple of years, but she came back.

Rita was the last of my biological siblings living. She
passed on a few years ago. Rita was about five years older
than me, so we weren't all that close growing up. But she
was always good to me when we saw each other. I'll always
remember that. We got closer as we got older. In the last few
years of her life she lived in the care home in Sagkeeng, so
I would drive there to visit her whenever I could.

My siblings became such an important part of my life as I
got older. It's hard to believe that in the early years of my life
I didn't even know they existed. I am grateful that I did get
to know them and that I was able to make some real
connections with my family. Many kids who are taken from
their homes and put into care never have that chance.

Not only was I adopted, but I never had to change my
surname. It was my biological dad's uncle John Morrisseau
and his wife Clara who adopted me. I called him Papa, but
he was actually my mishom, which means "grandfather" in
Ojibway. It was my adopted sister Virginia who explained it
all to me. Sometimes I wonder if maybe that's why he loved
and cared for me so much – because I was a blood relative.
I called my adopted mother Mama. She took good care of
me, but I never really felt loved by her. It was more my sister
Virginia who was like a mom to me. I also had my brothers
Alec, Fabian, and Melvin. Melvin was actually Virginia's son,
but my parents brought him up. They all saw me as their
sister, and I always considered them my brothers and sister
too. But like I said, Virginia was actually more of a mom to
me than a sister. She meant the world to me.

All the houses in my family were along that same old road. That's why the area is called Morrisseau Village. The big house where I grew up had two storeys. The outside was done in imitation brick. It had a big living room and grey linoleum floors. I remember I used to wax it and shine it all the time. It had wide stairs, and the whole second floor was just one big room. There was one partition down the middle of the room, and there were closets on either side. For the most part, we all slept up there, although there was a bedroom downstairs as well.

When I was young, we had a store in the house. I don't know how big the store was, but it couldn't have been that big. There were shelves in that big living room area, and I remember a counter with a cash register on it. I also remember a big bag of sugar with a little shovel in it. When someone came to buy some sugar, you had to scoop it into in a brown paper bag and weigh it. I'm thinking they sold sugar by the pound. There were also these big, see-through bowls filled with candy. But we never touched that candy.

I learned years later that my papa and his brother Albert owned the store and ran it together for quite some time. Then his brother started drinking too much and was drinking up the money, so my papa just let the store go. "Let him have it," he said. He gave his brother the store and it went down.

One of my earliest memories occurred around the time the store was closing. It came to me in a flashback. I remember seeing empty shelves. I understand that this happened in 1948, so I must have been about five or six years old. A lightning bolt ran straight through our house. I was standing on the main floor when I heard a very loud noise with lots of banging. I remember crying because I was so scared. I heard glass smashing, and looking to my right, I saw that window was smashed. There was nothing left. Apparently, that's where the lightning travelled through. I saw a baby on a baby swing, alone in that room. To this day I don't know who that baby was. This happened on a Sunday while my parents were in church, so no one else was around. After that, there were a lot of people that came there to see what happened. Even news people came to report on what had happened.

Around the time I started school, when I was about seven years old, my hair was split down the middle and was always combed back into braids. I guess I didn't like my hair split down the middle like that, so one day I decided to cut my hair myself. I cut the front part, so they had to cut it short to straighten my hair out. I had bangs after that and it looked better. My mama always made sure I was dressed well. It was important for me to dress nice and to have nice clothes, so that people could see that she was doing a good job looking after me. I remember I was always wearing dresses. When I went to school, I always had a good dress. My mama would get used clothing from the richer people in town and make things for me. I used to wear these black tunics with a white blouse underneath. It had a belt around the middle and a pleated skirt. I'd always wear these to school. I remember I had white and navy-blue shoes with laces. One year I had a zipper on my shoes, and I really liked those. I thought, "Oh man, I'm in style!" When I was about twelve years old, I had penny loafers. I bought my own stuff once I was able to work, but up until that point my mama always made sure I was dressed well.

My mama also used to take apart old jackets with a blade and cut them in squares to make blankets. There was this one time she made me a nice coat out of those old jackets. I remember that it was green and that she ripped it on the other side to make it look like a new jacket. She put buttons on it with a collar. It was so nice. She sewed it all herself with her old sewing machine. Those are the good memories, the ones that remind me of what she did for me. I learned how to be a good housekeeper from my mama, and I also learned to sew, cook, and clean by copying her. She was a good role model in that way.

My mama was a fair-skinned Scottish lady, but because of how long her family had lived in the community, she mostly talked Ojibway and some broken English. I remember that she had red hair before it turned grey. It was really long and copper-toned just like her dad's. When she was a young girl, her mother passed away, and her dad remarried this Native woman. Apparently, this woman was very, very mean to them. My mama worked really hard but was always being called down by her stepmom. She never received any love or hugs. She often talked about that and how they'd eat crumbs and leftovers off the table. So I came to understand why my mama was the way she was with me.

One hot summer day, when I was about five or six years old, I was playing outside while my mama was in the kitchen visiting with her friend. I hurt my foot and wanted comfort. I went crying to my mama.

My mama told me, "Go cry outside." But I sat under the table to be near her. I wanted her to look at my boo-boo, but she wouldn't. She ignored me, telling her friend in her Ojibway language, "She's a really bad and stubborn little girl."

All I ever wanted was her love. It was her saying that I was a bad kid that hurt more than anything. I cried more because she hurt my feelings, and not so much about the boo-boo on my foot. I remember so vividly how I felt at that moment. It was something that impacted me throughout my life. I always wanted my mama to love me, and I never felt that she did.

I would often see her showing love to my brother, Fabian. I thought that he was my real brother, before I found out I was adopted. I never understood what the difference was. I couldn't understand why she loved him and not me. When

I would see her showing love for him, I always wished that she would do that for me.

I don't remember very much about what Fabian was like when he was a kid. Like most brothers though, he could be kind of mean. Once we were playing outside together and he convinced me to go horseback riding. I was about seven at the time. We used the stairs by the wash line, and he sort of lifted me onto the horse's back. Then he slapped the horse and it reared, knocking me right off. Fabian was just laughing at me. My papa gave him heck for that.

Fabian had chores to do, like the rest of us. He was supposed to clean the barn, to take the manure and shovel it out. My papa used to get after him because he wouldn't listen. There was this one time when my papa came home and found that Fabian had been cooking for himself. He was eating in the kitchen when my papa came in. When my papa saw him there, he scolded him, "You know you were supposed to do your chores first before you did anything else." My papa would say things like that, but my mama always took up for Fabian. He used to get away with all kinds of things because of that.

Once, when I was about eight or nine years old, my brother Fabian and I were climbing on the roof of the barn. Our mama told us to get down. She threw something in our direction to get our attention. I think it was a stick. She hit my brother's leg by accident. He cried and came down. She cuddled and comforted him. I remember thinking, "I wish she would do that for me." I always wished that she would hold me.

She would sometimes give me really good lickings. I remember her telling someone how she used to get beatings from her mother too. I think that's probably why she treated me that way. Hitting someone was like a normal thing. It was normalized for me too. Still, I desperately wanted her to show me love and affection. I always tried to please her.

Nobody ever actually told me that I was adopted. I found out when I overheard my mama talking about it to one of her friends. She was telling them about the day they came to get us after my mother died. I felt confused and curious about what had happened, but it wasn't until I was much older that I asked any questions. Even then, it was my sister Virginia and my sister-in-law Annie that I spoke to. Annie was Alec's wife. They lived nearby, and I had a really good relationship with her. I was never able to talk with my mama the way I could with Virg or Annie.

After hearing that I was adopted, I finally began to understand why I always felt a deep loneliness. When I used to play with my friends Mimi and Bugsy, I would watch how their mother was with them and wonder. I loved their relationship with their mother and how she nurtured them. I used to ask myself, "I wonder what it feels like?" I felt a kind of loneliness because my mama wasn't my real mother, and I think I always had a sense of it, even before I knew. I always felt there was something missing in my life, and that's what it was I guess – a real mother.

Even if she wasn't my real mother, I still sought motherly love and affection from her. I wanted her approval and I always tried to please her. I was like that for the longest time with others too. I was always trying to please people. I now understand my own behaviours, where they came from and why I was the way I was, because of my understanding of human behaviour and trauma.

I never really had any bad feelings towards my mama for the way she treated me. I never blamed her. As I mentioned before, I believed that all of this was normal. Later, I came to understand it further when I learned about her upbringing, and I could empathize with her. So I don't hold anything against her. She did the best she could, even by just taking me in. I've learned to forgive.

My papa was different from my mama. I always felt loved by him, even though he never hugged me, held me, or even told me that he loved me. I just knew he loved me. My papa was a good man. I learned a lot of things by watching him and the way he lived. He was very generous and never expected anything in return. He was so kind to everyone. These things stay with you when you see them as a child. I share these things with clients that I work with, because it is so important for parents to know that their children are watching and learning from them all the time. To this day I try to be like my papa.

My papa was a slim, serious man. He always seemed to be concentrating, no matter what he was doing. Respect was very important to him. He didn't let us take large portions at meals. He would always say that people are hungry and that it was wrong to waste food. If we were still hungry when we had finished, then we could take more. He never talked when he ate, and I remember he even used to close his eyes when he ate, appreciating every bite.

My papa worked hard to provide for his family. He was a carpenter who used to build houses in the community during the summer. His main job, however, was that of a maintenance man at one of the schools. I'm not exactly sure which one. When he went off to work, he wore these grey striped coveralls. In the summertime I used to pick strawberries for him while he was at work in the morning. I would pick just enough for his dessert when he came home for lunch, mashing the berries and putting it on his bread or bannock.

One winter day, I was home with my sister Virginia, and I was sick. I don't know what was wrong with me, but I wasn't eating. She put some tomatoes and crackers in a bowl to have me try to eat something, but I just couldn't eat. So she got me ready to go to the Indian hospital in Pine Falls. She helped me put on my ski pants and did up the straps. The next thing

I remember is her carrying me to the car and her friend driving me to Pine Falls. We met my papa in front of the pool room and the barber shop with a blue, white, and red globe turning and spinning.

My papa took me to the old Indian hospital. I have memories of being there. It was very lonely, but I remember this one nurse who was very kind to me. I liked it when she was working. There was also a cleaning lady who used to give me an orange or sometimes an apple and would speak to me in Ojibway, telling me, "Don't let anyone see you eat it."

They were kind to me there, but I wasn't happy. I guess I used to cry by the window, watching and waiting for my papa to come and get me.

Then one day, as I was standing on the bed and watching for my papa to walk down the street, he came. He finally came to pick me up! I don't know how long I was there, only that it felt like a very long time. He brought a new dress for me when he came to pick me up. It was white with red strawberries and a red belt. I was so happy. I never needed my papa to hug me or to hold me and say, "I love you," because I always felt his love. I felt it in moments like this and in the lessons he taught me.

I have special memories of my papa coming home late on winter evenings and telling us stories. My brother Fabian and I would lay on the floor on either side of him by the coal burning Booker stove. This was before we had electricity. My papa would tell us these stories about Nanabozho. I remember that some of these stories were so long, and I would fall asleep listening to them. It's interesting that many of my childhood memories have been blocked out or have faded with time, yet I can still feel the warmth of that stove and the love of my papa as he told those traditional stories. The lessons I learned from them and from watching my papa have always stayed with me. They walk with me still because they have helped shape the person I am today and have sustained me through some impossibly difficult experiences.

I have some vague memories of Christmas as a child. I used to help my mama and Virg make Christmas pudding every year. To make that steam pudding they would mix up the ingredients and put it into these white sacks. Then they'd boil them for three hours. That was so awesome. The smell was amazing. I still make my Christmas pudding that way. It's a family tradition.

Once, when I was almost eight years old, my mama and papa took me to Winnipeg to go Christmas shopping. It was very early and my sister Virginia was still in bed when we left. As I was getting ready to go, she said in Ojibway, "Remind Papa to buy the record by Hank Williams. It's called *Weary Blues from Waitin'*." My brother Fabian also wanted a record by Hank Williams, but I can't remember the song. We used to have this big wooden record player. It was tall and had wooden legs on it, and you'd have to wind it up to play the records. I have nice memories of that. I think I forgot to tell my papa though. It was still dark out when my parents and I left to catch the bus to Winnipeg.

There were lots of Christmas lights in the city. We went into one store with squeaking floorboards. I don't remember what store it was though. My parents bought me a pair of winter boots that laced up and had fur around the edges. I just loved my new boots. It was such an exciting day. When we were coming home on the bus, my papa said, "Look, Diane." He was pointing to a red neon light in the shape of a man hitting something with an axe. The store was named Man with an Axe because they axed and lowered the prices. I don't remember getting home from this trip, but I do remember just how special it was.

As kids, my siblings and I had a lot of work to do, but we also had a lot of freedom. Most of our free time was spent outside. In the summer we used to take these big pails filled with water, and we used to go into the fields and fill the big gopher holes with water. The gopher would come up for air in different places. As kids we used to do that. We used to have a lot of fun playing.

Back then the river was clear and there were no weeds. Not like today. It was really nice. Sometimes, we'd spend the whole day swimming in that river. I also remember us swimming down there while Virg and my sister-in-law Annie would wash the clothes. They would have a fire going, and when they finished, we'd help them carry up the baskets to the line where they hung the clothes. When the weather wasn't so nice all the washing was done using water collected in these two big rain barrels that we kept by the house.

In the wintertime there used to be these big wide snow drifts. We used to make tunnels in them down by the bank where we lived. We never knew that those things could collapse. We didn't really think about danger at all back then. I loved to skate too. When the river froze it was clear and smooth, and I would be skating all the time. I would skate nearly all day until dark. I used to skate right across the river. Boy! I used to love skating. There were times when I was with other kids, but most of the time I was out there alone. No one ever talked to me about being by myself or asked me where I was. I could have fallen through the ice and drowned, but I was trusted to make good decisions on my own. We were taught lessons about respect, about nature and safety, through stories and observation. There was one area by the church where the river never really froze. It was always open water. It was a good thing I didn't skate over there. The thing is, I never had to be told not to skate there. I knew it wasn't safe. We all took risks, but somehow, we knew when a line shouldn't be crossed. There is a lot of research out there now on the benefits of risky play and

independence for children. Some people might think we
were being neglected, but I don't think so. There is wisdom
in giving kids freedom to take risks and to make mistakes.
And we weren't without limits or expectations. Especially
when it came to respecting others, my parents were strict.

There used to be a band hall in Sagkeeng that some of
us kids would play in. We were playing there this one time,
teasing this man, Frank, who had a developmental delay.
We weren't really being mean though. He was like a friend.
He was just laughing along with us as we were teasing him.
There was a man looking after the hall at the time. He came
over and told us to keep quiet. He told Frank to keep quiet
too. Frank became upset with that and grabbed him on the
shoulder and shook him. He was harmless, but I know that
man got really scared.

He was furious at all of us for that. So you know what
he did? He told my papa that I swore at him and used the
four-letter word. I never swore in those days. I think I must
have been about eight years old, and the others and I were
just kids being kids. We were having fun playing tag and
everything. We weren't really doing anything wrong or being
mean, just playing around. I can honestly say that I would
never have sworn at an adult back then. Still, that's what
he told my papa, and my papa believed him.

I was grounded for a week. I couldn't do anything. After
I would eat my supper and do the dishes and all my chores,
I had to go upstairs and stay there. This was during the
summertime, and it would be daylight up until ten o'clock
at night. I would hear and watch other kids playing baseball
and all of that from the window upstairs. When there was
about one day left in my punishment, I asked my papa,
"Can I go play outside now?" He told me, "If you ask me
again, you'll stay here for another week." So I never dared
ask again.

That's how my papa was. We never talked back or questioned him. I never talked back to him no matter what. I know it was love though. I have good memories of my papa because I knew that he loved me.

My parents never went to school and neither of them could read or write. My papa could sign his name though, and he taught my mama how to sign hers too. And even though we were poor, they always provided for us. We never went hungry. We ate so well back then. There was always good, fresh food, and my mama and Virg were really good cooks. I would look forward to lunch and supper coming home from school, especially when Virg was home. You could just smell her cooking coming through the door, making your mouth water. I think that's why I like cooking and baking to this day. The smell of Virg's cooking.

We had a big field of potatoes. I would get so excited when it was time to pick the potatoes. My papa would use the plow to turn the earth, and you'd see all these potatoes. Then we'd pick them and haul them back to the house. We had a big cellar where we kept our potatoes and other vegetables. Our vegetable garden was at the back of the house. I can still taste all the fresh vegetables we grew: corn, tomatoes, cucumber, radishes, and red beets. It was my job to help work in the garden and clean out the weeds. I used to like picking tomatoes and cucumbers, and I would help clean the peas. I loved being in the garden.

Along with working together in our garden, we used to go blueberry picking. It was something we did as a family. These are fond memories. There were lots of berries to pick in those days. It's not like today. You don't see many berry stands in Sagkeeng anymore, but there used to be a lot. There was this big field where we always used to pick berries. A highway goes through it now, and there are houses all around. There is still a small field still by the treatment centre, but back then there were no buildings at all there; just strawberries, raspberries, blueberries, and cranberries, all over. It's not surprising, then, that we had all kinds of jam all the time.

There was always plenty of meat as well. We had a barn and raised pigs, cows, and chickens. I remember going into the barn to collect the eggs. We used to eat chicken soup, or sometimes salt pork with white beans and bannock or loaf bread. It wasn't just farm animals though. My papa would hunt and trap as well. When the men would go hunting, they would always share the food. They knew who needed help. I remember this one woman, a single mother who had a few kids. My brother Fabian and my papa would take her deer meat and fish. My papa made his own boat, and he had lots of nets. I used to love eating fish the way my sister made it. She would boil the fish and serve it with potatoes and raw onion from the garden.

I have a distinct memory of my papa and Fabian coming home one day with a deer. I used to love the smell of Virg frying up that deer meat. She'd also cook up rabbits that my papa would bring home. She'd fry the meat with potatoes and onions. She always served it with fresh bannock too. I remember her taking off the cover and the steam just coming off it. My favourite part of the rabbit was the ribs. I would lick them just like a cat to savour the flavour after I'd finished.

There used to be a lot of water in that creek where we lived. It was deep and so dark. My papa used to put muskrat traps there. We used to bake and eat muskrats. They were so good. I used to like them. He just cleaned them, skinned them, and put them in the big oven. After you gut them, they look small, but they're good for you. My papa told us that they were healthy to eat because they eat stuff down under the water, like wee-kay (wild ginger). That's a medicine, wee-kay. It grows underwater and people pick it to help with things

like colds and sore throats. So it's healthy to eat muskrat
because they carry those medicines.

With both my parents working and our family growing
most of our own food, we were able to afford certain things
that a lot of others in the community couldn't. We were one
of the first families in Sagkeeng to have a television set. It was
a little black and white television, which was kind of snowy
sometimes. There were only about maybe three families on
the reserve that could afford to have a car, a telephone, and
a television during this period. People used to come to our
house to watch wrestling. They would come and set up their
chairs in the living room, and we had to make room. We
couldn't sit down. We always gave our neighbours a chair
to sit down and watch television. It was like a movie theatre,
and everyone was welcome.

My papa even had a car. I remember that it was black and
square. I think it was a 1949 model. There were times when
the roads would be really muddy after a rain, because there
were no gravel or paved roads on the reserve at the time.
Cars could easily get stuck, and it happened all the time. My
papa gave a lot of rides to people in that car. One day, this
woman asked him to take her to town. She wanted to give
him a dollar, which was a lot of money those days. My papa
wouldn't take the dollar.

He told the woman, "No, I don't need it right now. If
I need it, I will take it. You have children to feed." This was
all said in Ojibway. In those days everyone spoke the
Ojibway language. He was so generous and always giving,
never expecting anything in return. I learned these lessons
in generosity from my papa, and I always try to follow them
to this day.

That was how Sagkeeng was back then. It was a real
Ojibway-Anishinabe community. Come harvest time, all the
neighbours would get together to help each other out. They

used horse-drawn plows to cut the hay and pitchforks to pile it up. We would make bannock sandwiches and bring them to the fields. Everyone would stop to eat them and drink cold tea with milk. There was this one man who used to help my papa with the hay. After he passed away, my papa would share potatoes, deer meat, and moose meat with his widow; whatever we had, he would share with her. He also shared with others – anyone who needed help, he was there. That's just how it was back then. People took care of one another.

One time my little nephew, Alec's son, came over and wanted to help clean Kokum's garden. He was about three years old at the time. He just went in and cut all the corn down. It was only about three feet high, not at all ready. The grown-ups couldn't get mad though; he was trying to help. I remember them all laughing. He was only three, but already he was learning that value of helping others. It was an important part of who we were as a family, and as a community back then.

My sister Virginia was so important to me. There were happy times whenever she was home. She took good care of me. My sister Virginia was like a mom to me. Virg and I were always laughing and playing together. People tell me I used to like laughing. My sister used to say that I had a "sexy laugh." I didn't really know what that meant because I was too young. What I think she really meant, though, was that my laugh sounded good. It was a happy sound.

I was happy when we were together, but sometimes she would be gone for weeks, or months, and I remember being so lonely without her.

There was this one time she was gone for a long time. I think I was around seven or so, and I remember sitting by the window waiting for her. She was in the sanatorium because she had gotten sick with tuberculosis. Finally, she came home, but I didn't know if she was on leave for a visit or back for good. Years later, I found out that my papa had taken her out and was doctoring her himself with Anishinabe medicine. He made a drink to treat the tuberculosis. He would boil that medicine on our cookstove and put it in those big jars called sealers. Then he had my sister drink it like a tea every day until she was better.

Then one day the RCMP came dressed in uniform. They used to wear those black pants when they came onto the reserve. They came looking for my sister. I was so afraid that they would find her and take her away again, and of course they did. They took her back to the sanatorium because they thought she was still sick. I guess the medicine my papa made had really helped her though, and she was better, so they brought her home. Before long she started gaining weight back. After that she was herself again.

One of the family's pastimes in the evenings was playing cards. We had this big, round old-fashioned table. It looked like a pedestal to me. One evening, not long after Virg had recovered, I was sitting under that table while the rest of the family played cards. I think I was crying because I knew there was a guy waiting for my sister. I never liked that guy. I felt threatened by him because I was afraid that he would take my sister away again. I knew that she was going to leave just like the last time, and it broke my heart. I remember looking out the window as they left together and my papa telling me in Ojibway, "She's going to be back, but not right away." She left with her boyfriend, and they went to live in Red Lake, Ontario. Eventually she did come back, but by that time, she had two little boys. I felt a deep sadness when she left. I guess I must have been grieving, which I recognize now because I've grieved many losses in my life since.

My sister taught me a lot when she was home. I was about ten or eleven years old when I started to learn how to make bannock by watching my sister Virginia make it. I would

come home from school at lunchtime, and it was mainly my
sister who would make me lunch. Often, she would make
soup, which was delicious, but I loved it best when she cooked
rabbit in the frying pan. We had fresh bannock all the time,
which she cooked using an old wood stove. It felt so good
when she was home. It was a real home then. Our place was
always clean, and she cooked nice meals. There was always
soup and bannock in the house when she was home. I knew
that she loved me, and when she left, I had to learn to survive
on my own. She taught me how to cook and clean at an early
age. I was determined to learn. I had to learn!

My sister-in-law Annie was there for me, too, and she
taught me other important skills when Virginia wasn't there.
She also made bannock and loaf bread really well. I remember
when I first tried making loaf bread, it would always go flat.
My papa told me once, "Diane, stop spoiling that flour and
just make bannock." I didn't give up though. The next time
I tried to make bread and it didn't turn out right, I hid a
bunch of that dough outside so my papa wouldn't see!

I couldn't figure out what I was doing wrong. Annie was
the one who pointed out the problem. I guess I had used hot
water, and that cooked the yeast too early. She taught me,
"Everything has to be lukewarm. The water and oil have to be
lukewarm so that the yeast doesn't cook right away. That's
why your bread doesn't rise." Finally, I was able to make loaf
bread! It was nice. I learned to be domestic. It's not like
today because now everything is so easy. You can buy just
about anything already made and hardly have to lift a finger.

You know, I thought it was normal to be called lazy. It
didn't matter what I did or how hard I worked; this was how
my mama saw me. I remember working hard at the things
I learned. By the time I was twelve years old I was hauling
water, washing, and scrubbing the floors and clothes all day.
My mama and papa worked in town, so I was also expected

to make supper. I would often make soup and bannock. I worked hard but it was never enough. I didn't realize or know that it wasn't like this for most people. I thought it was normal.

It was my sister-in-law who brought it to my attention many years later. She told me, "I felt sorry for you." When Annie used to come over to use the phone or visit, she would see me working in the house. She said, "You worked hard all day. I saw you hauling water, hanging clothes, and then ironing clothes after you cleaned up the house. And then I would hear your mama calling you lazy because you forgot to wash the little boys' faces." She would get really upset about that kind of thing. I realized then that maybe the way I was treated wasn't normal. Still, I never felt any resentment towards my mama. She did the best she could, and maybe she thought this was normal too. I found forgiveness for her.

I had to work hard growing up, but so did my parents, and I was well provided for as a young child. I was dressed in the best clothes my family could afford. I had good food to eat. I had a father who loved me and protected me. I learned these lessons about how to work hard and how to treat others from my mama and papa. I might have lacked motherly love and affection at the time, but I truly thought that this was normal. In fact, I thought I came from a relatively perfect home.

I can remember a lot of good things about my childhood. But there were some horrible things happening around me and to me during this time. Things that for the most part, I blocked out. I have no real memory of some things. There are clues, signs, and certain behaviours I had that hinted at the truth, but for years I could not see or understand them. Memories hidden in the protective shadows of the mind are still memories, still have an impact on your inner thoughts and feelings, on your actions and decisions. This was my experience.

When I began my healing journey, I started looking into my past to try and understand what happened to me. One of the more disturbing things I learned is that one of the people who looked after me before I was adopted by my mama and papa was a pedophile. I'm not sure how many days or weeks I was fostered in this home. I think that it is very likely my first experience with abuse happened there, when I was just an infant. I've been having flashbacks of something happening to me as a baby. In one of these flashbacks, I see a big figure standing over me. I was crying and kicking. I don't know what happened. Maybe I'm not ready for this one specific memory. Maybe it's just too much.

My first flashbacks started a long time ago, after my sister Virginia shared some things from our childhood with me. She really helped me through the hard times in my life. I shared a lot with Virginia when she'd come and visit through the years. She would share some of her memories and experiences with me as well. We would just sit and talk for hours. There was this one time when we were talking about my husband Edgar, and the conversation turned to our childhood.

Edgar was very jealous and would often accuse me of being with other men before him. I said to Virg, "You know, it's strange: I never, ever went to bed with another guy before him, but somehow, I know I wasn't a virgin either. That's why he used to always beat me up. He knew I wasn't a virgin. Maybe that's why he treated me that way," I added.

She looked at me funny then, and I asked, "Why are you looking at me like that?"

"Maybe something happened to you as a kid."

"Yeah, maybe," I said.

Virg said, "Something happened to me too. That's why I put myself in school."

I was somewhat surprised to hear this. "I didn't even know you were in residential school," I told her.

"Yeah. I left home because of it. Mama never listened to me, and that's why I put myself in school." She went on, "I thought it was just me, but it might have happened to you too."

Virg thought she saw something being done to me. She told me that one day she went upstairs, and she saw a man walking away from one of the beds zipping up his pants. She said there was a little girl lying on the bed that he was walking away from. I was the only little girl in the house at the time, so it had to be me. She was vague about it when she told me. She probably knew more, but maybe she didn't think I could handle it. I started having flashbacks after my sister shared this stuff with me. In this one flashback I saw someone over me. He was wiping my legs. I had blood all over them. I could see that I had little shoes on. I was so small and scared. My body felt sick. I threw up after seeing that.

I don't know who abused me. There were always men coming and going in and out of our house; like this one guy, who would come and just watch me as I was cleaning the house. He had a reputation. He used to show kids his privates.

Then there was another man who was caught molesting a young girl many years later. I have one memory of when I was about seven or eight years old, maybe. This man showed some of us kids his privates, and he was trying to lie on top of me. Two other men were there too. These guys all used to be in the residential school, and I think that they were probably abused there too. Where else would they have learned that? I got away and I tried to tell my mama what they were doing. She called me a liar and she wouldn't believe me. So I knew I could never tell her anything after that. Virginia understood how I felt. She never felt heard and was never believed either. For the longest time we both thought our mama knew what was happening but didn't care.

Virg told me about the time she realized I was probably being abused too. "Mama brought you to the school one time to come and visit me. You were limping, walking funny, and I asked Mama what was wrong with you. She didn't say, but I knew something was wrong with your private area."

"I wonder if she took me to the hospital?" I asked.

"I don't think so."

There were signs of abuse, which nobody saw or wanted to see. Maybe they just didn't know what to do. I remember wanting to masturbate as a very young child. I have one memory of looking for something to use, to put inside me. Obviously, somebody taught me that, but I don't know who. I was only a little girl, but I knew things about sex. I understand where those ideas came from now.

I also remember a time when I was about seven years old, and our cousins came to visit. They lived in the white community, and they spoke only English. I didn't know how to speak English, but we still played together. This one time, I was playing sex with my cousin, and my mama walked into the room and caught us playing. I don't know where my papa was when that happened. Probably at work. Anyway, it was my mama that saw us, and it was my mama that punished me. I got a really good strapping. I thought she was never going to stop hitting me and that I was going to die. I remember that. I remember sitting on the wooden boards of the second floor of our house. I remember just sitting there, looking at my legs, and they were just so swollen from the gum rubber she used to strap me. She called me a dirty little girl in Ojibway. I still remember that. I was crying. It's like a dream.

I think when my mama beat me that day, she might have cured me of thinking that way because I don't think I ever did anything like that ever again. Sometimes I think maybe it was a good thing my mama half killed me because, who knows, I might have become a perpetrator too. Professionals in the area point out that those who were abused might abuse others as well. They say you can become one, do things to others that happened to you. I'm thankful that nothing like that ever happened to me. I never thought that way. Looking back, I thought that in some ways she helped me, because it showed me that what was done to me wasn't normal – that it was wrong. But by ignoring my cries for help and beating me, she really hurt me. I felt alone and ashamed.

Having Virg made me feel less alone, and it had such a profound impact on me and my healing journey when she told me about what happened to her. It was many years later before we were able to talk openly like this, but I can only imagine the good it would have done if someone had noticed, believed me, and helped me back then. Children need to be heard, to know that they are not alone. This is why I feel it's important that I share my story, even these parts that are hard to face. It is painful to talk about, and I know it will make people uncomfortable. Maybe this is why so many parents and caregivers react the way my mama did when I tried to tell her what happened to me – the truth is so terrible, the discomfort so great, that they close themselves off to the possibility. It is understandable, but in doing this they close themselves off from the child and what they are experiencing. The child is left to suffer in silence and shame. That was my experience, and it was years into my adulthood before I felt safe enough to start facing what happened to me. I couldn't have done it alone. Having one trusted adult can make all the difference. That's one thing I want people to take from my story: to have the courage to believe kids and be there for them, help them, even when it is hard and scary.

2

Day School

I ATTENDED THE DAY school in Sagkeeng. The truth about
what happened in residential and day schools all over the
country is finally coming out, finally being acknowledged.
But it's not enough. Things are still not right. My own
experience with the process was another kind of hell for me.
The government is giving compensation for the abuses that
took place in residential and day schools, as if that makes
things right. Some people are getting a lot of money for
what they went through, but I didn't get what I should have.
I couldn't tell them all that happened to me in that school.
A lot of things are still blocked for me, and when I tried to
share what I do remember, I got so violently ill I had to stop.
So I had to walk away with less compensation than I should
have. What's worse, I had to walk away feeling unheard, yet
again. I will be heard though. I will share what I am ready to
share here and hope that it helps give some insight into the
decisions I made; the struggles I faced, especially as a parent;
and the person I was and who I am today.

My papa was strong, and he was smart. When those men
came to get us, he said, "I've taken care of my kids all these
years. We don't need you." They came twice, but he stood up
to them. He said, "They're not going to live there. They will

go to school. We live close enough, they can walk every day."
I must have been around six or seven when I started school.
I was small for my age. That was when I wore my hair in
braids before I cut it and got bangs. I always had red or
sometimes green ribbons at the ends of my braids. It was
only about a quarter of a mile to the school from my house,
so I was able to walk to and from school, and I went home
for lunch every day. I had an hour, and sometimes my older
sister Virginia would be there with a nice hot meal of soup
and bannock for me. I was always very grateful for that.

I attended school in the one-room day school house the
first year. It was intimidating. Sister Matilda was one mean
teacher who would hit us with a strap or a big ruler. Going
to school was very scary, especially when you didn't speak the
language. I didn't know English when I started school. My
first language is Ojibway and that's all we talked at home. So
it was scary, especially when you had to use the washroom.
They didn't let you go if you didn't ask in English. One time,
I peed myself because I couldn't remember the words. That
Sister Matilda made fun of me. She was clapping her hands
and laughing along with the other kids. I just stood there,
scared and ashamed. That was my first and last experience
with that. I didn't want it to happen to me again, so I would
just run out and go to the washroom when I had to. I would
get hit because I didn't ask permission, but I didn't want to
be humiliated like that again.

I watched it happen to other kids, too: peeing themselves
and pooping themselves, too, and being humiliated because
of it. I remember one time a boy went up to the front of the
room and said to Sister Matilda, "I wanna shit." He wasn't
being rude; he just didn't know the right word to use. He
got supreme heck for that. He was told, "Go and sit down
until you learn to ask properly." His older sister was in the
classroom and maybe could have helped him, but he was too

humiliated to do anything. He just sat down and eventually he dirtied himself, of course. He just sat there crying. I was two desks away from him. We had those double desks with the chairs that would fold up. I can still remember the smell. Slowly, I learned how to speak a few words in English, like "washroom," so I wouldn't have to just run out anymore.

There were a lot of bullies in the school, and Sister Matilda deliberately placed me in situations where I was exposed to that violence. She would always make me hang my coat where those bullies were, and she used to sit me in the place next to this girl who was very mean to me. We got into a fight this one time, and Sister Matilda was standing there clapping. She was just watching us and clapping her hands while we fought. I had a lot of rage already at that age, and I fought back when I was picked on. I grabbed that girl by the hair and bumped her face on the desk. It made her nose bleed, and that might have been the end of it, but she grabbed my hair, too, and I remember my neck was so sore and my head felt heavy after that fight. Sister Matilda wouldn't stop us. She was getting a kick out of it, laughing and clapping her hands. I knew even then that she knew what she was doing, that she deliberately put me there.

Sister Matilda didn't like me because of the things that I did, like running out of the class to go to the washroom. I was stubborn because I knew that what she was doing was wrong, even as a child. It didn't take long before I had it up to my neck with all the violence that happened in school, and she was behind a lot of it. There would always be big fights in school because of those bullies. There were bullies even then, but the adults in the school weren't there to help us or protect us from them. In fact, they encouraged the bullying. I remember never feeling safe. She could have stopped it and protected me, but she didn't. I remember those girls who used to bully me. They were all cousins and relatives. One time they all stood in two lines out in the playground. They made me walk down the middle of the lines, and they got their little sister to kick me. Sister Matilda was watching everything. That young girl kicked me, but I grabbed her, and she fell on the ground. Then I just stood there, and I looked at everybody, all those girls. I thought they were going to gang up on me, but I was ready. Nobody made a move.

Years later I was talking to one of my friends who went to that school with me. She said, "We were already adults." In many ways she was right. We were taking care of ourselves already. She said to me, "Did you know that even the big girls were scared of you in school?" I didn't know it then, but I do know why now. They were afraid of me because of my rage. Even at that young age, they were afraid of me. I never looked for a fight, but I defended myself, and I stood up for the smaller kids too.

When I started in the bigger school, I thought it would be better. In some small ways it was, but in others it was much, much worse. I was bullied less in the big school. I used to have a black tunic that my mama brought back from a family she worked for in town. The white people would give her hand-me-downs from their kids, from their daughters. So I had these black tunics and white blouses, and I wore stockings with good shoes. The other girls in the school used to say that they admired my stockings. They had to wear these real thick, ugly stockings. So they liked the way that I dressed. I remember that. It felt good to be admired.

The other thing that was different was that I wasn't alone in that big school. One time this girl tried to fight me. I was in grade two, close to when I started at that big school. There was a big room downstairs with benches all around the wall where students would put their skates and their shoes and whatnot. You could open the benches along the wall and keep your things in them. If I remember correctly, I think

I was in that girl's way, and she got mad at me. It was my sister Rita who came to my rescue. Rita was four years older than me, so if I was eight, she must have been about twelve. She seemed like such a big girl to me because she was older, and besides, she was always kind of a chubby girl. Rita went straight up to that girl and said, "Leave her alone. You know, she's way smaller than you and you're not going to do that. I'm her big sister." It really felt good that I had someone who cared about me, who was willing to take up for me when this big girl tried to fight me and intimidate me. Up to that point I was always alone, and I didn't really have anyone, so that felt really good. That girl never bothered me again.

I used to go to school early in the morning sometimes, and I would see the other students having breakfast in that big room. I think it was called the Rectory. There were rows of tables where the boys and girls would eat. The girls were on one side and the boys were on the other side. Before breakfast they made everybody line up to drink castor oil. I guess they had to take that for health reasons, but it tasted awful. They made me line up a couple of times, too, since I was there. The first time I tasted it I spat it right out. I got hit for that. The next time, I wouldn't open my mouth. I closed my lips tight, and that sister slapped me on the head and just pushed me out of the way. I guess she didn't force me because I was not a resident there anyway.

There were a whole bunch of different nuns there. I don't remember all their names. I remember one sister though; we called her Sister Weeass. She was short and fat, but she wasn't too bad. She wasn't that mean. I'd see her laughing and making fun of us, but I thought, "You know what? That's not too bad." Others were mean. I remember one nun was really bad. I think her name was Sister Leonard.

She was the nun that locked me up. I'll never forget that. It was very traumatizing. I thought I was going to die in there. She locked me in the basement washroom. It had about four or five green stalls and the same number of sinks. The floors looked like marble, but they were concrete. I remember looking up at the one tiny window and thinking, "My body will be rotten before my papa finds me." That's what I thought. I thought I was going to die in there. I remember I lay on the floor, and I was kicking that door really hard with the heels on my shoes. I kicked and screamed for my life. Years later my sister told me they could hear me screaming from the third floor.

I don't know how long I was in there for, but it seemed like forever. Finally, they opened the door. By that time my body was limp. Those nuns grabbed my wrists and dragged me out. They started swinging me. Eventually they let me go, and I fell flat on the floor. I remember seeing that floor up close. It was where we used to have recess. It had little wooden boards. If I remember correctly, they let me go, and moving quickly on my hands and knees I grabbed one of those nuns around her legs and I bit her. She had on black shoes with laces and heels, maybe two-inch heels or something like that. I bit her hard. I must have looked like a little dog! The other one pulled me away by the feet, then grabbed hold of me while the other nun was hitting me. That was a bad beating, but getting a licking like that wasn't nearly as terrible as being locked in that bathroom. That was really traumatizing.

I went home every day, but it didn't stop the abuse. My sister Rita told me one time, "Even though you were not in the boarding school, you experienced more abuse than I did." I could never tell my parents. We weren't ever allowed to tattle tale, and that's what they said it was. More than that, though, I thought to myself, "How can I tell them about these really bad things happening to me? They see these people as holy people. Servants of God! They're never going to believe me." My mother had said I was a liar already before, when I tried to tell her something bad that happened when I was little, so I didn't feel safe telling her anything. I guess that's why I kept it to myself all those years. I couldn't tell anyone.

There were these two nuns who were really nice to me in the beginning. I don't even remember their names. I wasn't the only one either; there were other girls that got that special treatment too. They were always giving us food and nice things to eat, like cupcakes. The one nun would keep us after school to help and would pay us with jellybeans or fruit. She had oranges, grapes, and other fruits in a basket for us. Eventually, I trusted her. Now I understand that she was grooming me. I didn't understand it then. I thought she liked me, and I was so desperate for any kind of affection. It wasn't long before she started taking me into a little back room and abusing me. At first, I thought I was the only one, but the sexual abuse happened to other kids too. I saw other girls being abused too. I saw a priest or brother feeling up girls by the kitchen area, towards the furnace room. I witnessed that sort of thing so many times.

During the summer holidays, I used to go to the school to play with the kids that didn't go home. They were usually the ones who came from far away, or who didn't have any parents. There were quite a few kids from Berens River and Bloodvein, and I was good friends with one of them from Berens River. I used to go to the school and play with those girls, especially my one friend. We'd play for hours on the swings, the teeter-totter, and the fire escape. My parents were always working in town and so they never missed me when I came home late.

Years later, I was talking with someone I went to school with, and she revealed something else that happened to me. That girl asked me, "You remember how we used to pick bugs in the potato field by the school?"

I said, "Yeah, we used to have to pick these bugs off the potato plants. We'd put them in baking powder tins. I remember."

She said she'd seen a few girls abused by the farmer. She named him, but I don't remember who she said he was. "You were one of them," she said.

I don't remember that at all. Not at all. But I do remember going into the big barn with another girl, and this guy had oranges. He was trying to give us an orange, but that's all I remember. I have no doubt that something must have happened though. It seems I was always being victimized that way.

During the summer, the nuns would invite me into the school and would allow me to have a bath because we didn't have running water back then. At the time we were still using rainwater that was collected in two big barrels. Or sometimes the water man used to deliver water. We used to have to warm up the water for cleaning, dishes, and things like that. At the school they had those big old-fashioned tubs and lots of hot water. It was those same two nuns who used to take me into that back room. I thought they really liked me. I understand now they were grooming me, brainwashing me. I remember the first time it happened, I felt so sick. But it was nice to have a hot bath, to feel clean and cared for.

The sexual abuse started my first year going to the big school, and it went on until I was about eleven or twelve. Then they didn't like me anymore. It turned exclusively to physical and emotional abuse. I couldn't learn in school. I never completed grade seven. I was ashamed because by the time I was fourteen, almost fifteen, I was still only in grade seven. I had so much pain and rage that I couldn't learn anything. I understand now it's because of all the trauma, the abuse as a child, why I couldn't learn. It's almost like having a learning disability because of what happened.

It takes a lot out of you. You don't feel normal. Kids like me are often treated like failures. Thankfully, awareness is increasing about how toxic stress and trauma impact learning and development. I'm hopeful that as educators and social workers begin to use trauma-informed practices in their work, fewer children will experience the shame that I did and more will recognize their potential sooner.

I was fifteen years old when I fought back and walked out of class for good. I never went back. I was in class on the second floor where the grade six and seven classrooms were. It was all girls in that class. Sister Dummy was teaching us that day. I remember her, she had buck teeth. She wanted us to sing in Latin and was standing there, waving her hand for us to sing. She had her finger pointed in the air, but nobody sang. We didn't know that language. She got mad, and she told us, "Go to sleep, you lazy Indians."

So everybody went down, with their heads down on their desks. I did, too, but I could see out the window from where I sat, and I saw my papa walking across the field. I lifted my head maybe a couple of inches to see him better. I guess Sister Dummy saw that. She came walking towards me fast; I could hear her footsteps. She hit me in the head with a book as hard as she could. My forehead banged on the desk with the force of that book. I had a bump on my forehead, and I remember seeing little sparks when she hit me. I remember that so clearly.

I jumped up and I swung my fist at her. "You fucking bitch!" I screamed.

She moved back quick, and I think she stepped on her big black veil. The white veil thing on top of her head went sideways. She grabbed it right away because it almost fell off her head. She went running towards the door and opened it to leave. I was so angry that I went running after her. I was going to beat her up, and she was scared. But I changed my mind. I just walked out of the class. I was done. I went straight to my papa's shop, and I told him I was going home and would never go back.

A week or two later I went to evening services at the church with my family, and Sister Superior approached me outside the church after the service.

She said, "You can come back to school now. Sister forgave you."

I thought, "I'm the one who needs forgiveness? It was the other way around!" I was more pissed off than before.

I was already fed up with the church by that point. I had stopped wanting to go to church by the time I was twelve. I'd see them preaching up there, and knowing how they treated us kids, I was just filled with rage. They were so mean to us in school, and then in front of our parents they'd talk nice to us, act nice. I didn't know the word then, but they were hypocrites. I couldn't listen to the priest up there talking about spirituality and all that, knowing what they were doing in the school. After Sister Superior talked to me that evening, I made up my mind I wouldn't go to church anymore either.

When I decided not to go back to school or church, my mama was really upset. She used to say things and try to manipulate me to go, but I was stubborn. My papa never forced me to go back to school or church, and he didn't make me feel bad about it either. Years later, I overheard my papa praising me to a friend of his. He said that I was a hard worker, and he talked about that time I walked out of school. He was telling his friend, "She was strong enough, and honest enough, to come and talk to me and say she was leaving school."

So that's one of the reasons why I think, "I wonder if he knew?" My parents must have known something, but I don't know. I never told anyone what I went through there because

I thought no one would believe me. So many people were going to that church, believing these people, believing that they're good people. I knew then that it was wrong, and I didn't want to be dishonest like them. I couldn't say anything, but I wasn't going to act like everything was okay either. I'm like that to this day. I'm not a phoney person. I don't pretend nothing.

The nuns used fear on all of us. They used God. They said things like, "You're not going to go to heaven if you don't do this." They used manipulation to control us all those years, putting fear into us so that they could get what they wanted, abusing us for their own satisfaction. Fucking pigs. For years and years, I suffered. To this day I carry the shame and guilt they planted in me.

It is that shame that never gets talked about. That shame that comes to a child, desperate for affection, who can't help but enjoy that feeling of being wanted. I enjoyed it. I liked having a bath there, and what they did to me felt like affection at the time. I was ashamed of that for so many years. That's why I buried it for so long. I know I didn't like it at first, but then I remember looking forward to it. I carried this shame and guilt for most of my life, without understanding where the shame was coming from because the memories were buried so deep. I am not alone in this experience of abuse and undeserved shame. What I went through as a child made me vulnerable, a prime candidate for men like Edgar to prey upon. If I had known what real love felt like, if I had security and confidence, I would have seen things so differently. I probably never would have looked his way.

I am not sharing any of this to shock or offend anyone. I just want people to know the truth, the whole, ugly truth, and to know that it is possible, even in the worst of circumstances, to survive, to heal, and eventually to thrive. I am living proof that it is possible. I am proud of who

I am and where I am now in my life, and that is not despite what I went through but because of it. I use what I went through to help others, and I hope that sharing my story will educate and inspire others to do the same. And most importantly, I hope that sharing my story will help those suffering in silence to speak. Because you are not alone and you are worthy of being heard.

3

Posting of the Bands

SOMETIMES I THINK I didn't really have much of a childhood at all because of all the trauma and abuse I experienced. Besides that, I had too many responsibilities to have many normal childhood experiences. I started working around the house when I was really young. I always tried to please my mama. I cleaned, washed clothes, ironed, babysat, and did anything else I was told to do. It hurt that she never really showed me any appreciation, but I'm still grateful for all that she taught me. I know that I am a good housekeeper and a hard worker in large part because of her.

When I was twelve, I started going with my mama to help her clean houses in town. I'm not sure how I felt about it at the time, but I don't remember disliking it. I was used to hard work already, and sometimes I would even make a little money. Every once in a while, she'd give me five dollars for the work I did, and I learned a lot. Eventually, she started letting me clean houses on my own. She would bring me there and tell me what I needed to do, and I began to work by myself. At the time they paid six to ten dollars a day to clean houses in Pine Falls. Sometimes I'd make myself ten whole bucks if I worked all day in a house by myself. That early start gave me more independence, and it helped prepare me for the adult responsibilities I would have all too soon.

When I left school I started working as much as I could. I couldn't work every day because I was still expected to keep up with my work at home. My first job, aside from helping my mama clean houses, was babysitting. This lady paid me to take care of her two sons while she went to work. They were too young to attend school, I think around four and five years old. Sometimes she would pay more if I did other chores, too, like ironing their clothes. It wasn't too different from the work I did at home, so I liked it.

Before too long I also started working weekends at the Pine Falls restaurant with my mama, who was working as a cook there. Sometimes I would help in the front, but mostly I would help in the kitchen with my mama. I already knew how to make bannock and soup by the time I was twelve, so it was easy. I didn't mind helping and I got paid too. When I was fifteen I started waitressing, and I was making about thirty-four dollars every two weeks. That was a lot of money in those days. Sometimes I gave my mama and papa part of my little paycheques. Seventeen dollars or so here and there to help with the bills. I wanted to help. The rest I got to keep for myself, and I was happy with that.

I always worked hard and never really had time to go out with my friends. Sometimes though, if I didn't have to work and my papa let me, I would go to a baseball game. There were baseball games in the field next to the church on Sundays, or in the evenings during the week. I'd go there and just walk around with my friends, talking and laughing. They smoked, and because I always had money, working the way I did, and because my friends never had money, they would try and get me to buy smokes for them. I didn't though because I didn't smoke. I still don't know where they ended up getting them. I tried it once, but I didn't like it. We may have been different, but we always had fun together.

My best friends at the time were Mimi and Bugsy. I hung out with them some Sundays and whenever I was off from work. Mimi, Bugsy, and I used to walk to their house, which was about two miles from mine. I remember thinking they had a nice place. Their house had these nice grey floors with some kind of fancy pattern, and they had a floor model record player. We played 45 records and would dance to the music for hours. I loved to dance. We had a lot of fun. Their parents usually weren't home. Like my parents, they were always working, or at the hall by the Catholic church, where there was always something going on. I think they were involved in fundraising for the church too.

I was about thirteen when I started going out with my friends like that. It was also around that time that I started having problems with my brother Joseph. Joseph had never really liked me, but things got worse as I got older. I was scared of him. He started to punch me randomly for no apparent reason. One time I met him in the hall as he was going down the stairs and I was coming up them. He just punched me. It knocked me over and I went rolling down the stairs. I was so hurt.

He didn't treat Juliana that way. He was nice to Juliana, always buying her nice things. I remember he bought her a nice yellow blouse once. I don't know where he was working. He was working somewhere, and he made money and bought her stuff. He was never good to me, but once he actually bought me a camera, and another time he got me a blouse. I think he felt guilty about the way he treated me. I was always scared of him, trying to dodge him all the time.

I was sweeping up one time and Joseph walked by and just punched me in the head. Fabian saw what happened, and he told him, "Leave her alone, boy." Just like that. He was trying to protect me. Joseph made a threatening gesture, like he was going to punch Fabian. He was very angry, and I think that scared Fabian. I was grateful to Fabian for standing up for me like that.

I never understood why Joseph treated me the way he did. It was my sister-in-law Annie who told me, "I think he's jealous of you just like a girlfriend." I was confused by this, but I just brushed it off. I didn't think too much of it at the time.

But then he started talking about weird things. He said things like, "Did you know that some of our cousins have sex together?"

I thought, "Ew. Why would he say that?" I really didn't know why he would talk like that. I was kind of naive then. I guess he was trying to make me think that way, to make it seem normal.

One time I came home after being out with some of my friends, and that blouse he had bought me was cut up. That's when it made sense to me. I thought, "Yeah, he must be jealous." I was worried and wanted to tell my mama that there was something wrong with him, but I knew she would never believe me, so I kept my fears to myself.

Later that same year, I opened my drawer to change my clothes and there was a note. It was from my brother Joseph. It was a confession. He wrote to tell me that he was leaving. He had spoken to the priest, I think it was Father Plammadon, about his feelings towards me. He confessed to the priest, and then to me in that letter, that he had sexual urges towards his own sister – towards me. He wrote in there that he used to take my covers off and look at me when I was sleeping. He explained that the Father advised him to leave before anything happened. I felt sick to my stomach, knowing that he was my brother and had those feelings about me. I never really felt safe when he was around, and now I knew why.

Not long after reading his letter I was upstairs washing the wooden floors. I thought I was home alone, but he came in and he punched me hard. Then he raped me. My own brother. Afterwards, he left for Winnipeg to stay with our sister, and that was the end of that. He was gone.

After he left, I didn't have to feel afraid anymore. But I felt dirty and guilty. I never told anyone what he did. It affected me for a long time. After that, I always made sure I went to sleep fully covered. I used to go to bed fully dressed with my jeans and my blouse on, or make sure I had long pyjamas. I never wore anything short after that. As a teenager I didn't like to wear shorts or skirts because I didn't want guys to look at me. Even in my relationships with men years later as an adult, I didn't want to show my body because of that. That's how much I was affected by what had happened.

When I got a little older, my friends and I started going out more often. Some of them were kind of wild though, and I really wasn't into a lot of the stuff they were doing. They'd have boyfriends with cars, and they'd drive around with them. Sometimes they'd try to pick me up, but I didn't go with them because I wasn't allowed. My papa tried to protect me from that kind of lifestyle. Those friends are not living today. Too much alcohol. I know of at least one of them that died because of that.

My papa was strict. When he said something, he stayed with it. We had a phone that was on the wall. It was a party line. We had a certain ring if the call was for us. My papa never allowed us to talk to our friends on there. One time, I was talking to my friend, and he said, "Get off that phone! That's not for entertainment." So I was trying to get my friend off the phone. I said, "I have to go." But she kept on talking. My papa just grabbed the phone and hung it up. I thought he was so mean sometimes, my papa. But he was just strict. Respect was so important to him, and he knew that people might need to use the phone to make an important call. I always did what he told me to, and I never talked back to him. When I got older I wouldn't even smoke in front of my papa. I respected him too much.

At fourteen years old I met Edgar. There had been some other guys that tried to go out with me before then, but I wasn't interested in any of them. So until Edgar I had never had a boyfriend or gone on any dates. I knew of Edgar before we actually met. He came from Scanterbury, another reserve about forty minutes south of Sagkeeng. His sister was our neighbour, and he would come around pretty often. He was nineteen, and I thought he was good-looking and charismatic. He had black hair that he combed back like Elvis Presley. He tried to imitate him, I guess. He used to wear a yellow James Dean jacket, and that first summer we were dating he was going around wearing red pants. The young girls were crazy over him in Sagkeeng. I thought it was cool at first. After a while it turned me off, but by then it was kind of too late.

There was a movie theatre at the hall on the reserve at that time. My friends and I used to walk over there and go to the movies sometimes. That's where I first met him. He walked me home that first night. It was wintertime and I remember he had on a white jacket, like a car coat. He was drunk and falling all over the place, but I didn't mind. I didn't think anything about drinking at the time. I was used to it. Edgar had started drinking when he was really young, and he was nearly twenty by then. As we walked along in the dark, he was holding me by the waist.

He looked at me and asked, "How old are you?" I was going to be fifteen in three months, so I said I was fifteen. I lied to make myself older because I wanted him to like me.

He said, "Too young." I felt disappointed. I didn't realize this was part of his strategy. Edgar preyed on young girls.

Despite what he said about my being too young, he would come around on the weekends in his dad's light blue half-ton and pick me up sometimes. He and his friends were always picking up girls around there. One time I saw the truck with the word *Casanova* written on it in red lipstick. He told me that some girls wrote that stuff with their lipstick. I knew that he was dating other girls, but it didn't really bother me at the time. Even my friend Mimi used to go out with him. We were best friends, and she used to say, "Oh, there he is in his truck driving around again." She would say to me, "I'll go out with him this weekend. You already went out with him last weekend." And I'd say, "Okay, then." We were just young girls having fun.

Some of the other girls seemed to be jealous of me and would say things about me. I think it was partly because I had nice clothes too. I worked and would buy clothes from The Bay in town. I remember I had black and red pedal-pushers and nice blouses that I bought for myself with the money I earned at my different jobs. They were also jealous over Edgar. I never felt jealous or even hurt about what they said though. I guess I didn't really care what they said. I was having fun and didn't take any of it too seriously.

That first summer, on a Sunday afternoon, Edgar and his friend picked me and my friend up to go driving. We spent the afternoon sitting on the rocks by the river, talking and just hanging out. Later, we went to where the train was by the paper mill in Pine Falls. He got me to climb on top of the parked train. We walked on top of them for fun. After that, he drove past my place and parked. We talked for a bit, and he kissed me goodnight before he dropped me off at my house. It felt nice to be with him, but I felt a bit intimidated. The next time I saw my friends they told me that he went back to pick up another girl that night. Still, it didn't really bother me too much at that point. Honestly, I didn't really want to be his girlfriend because of what he was like. He was very aggressive.

One evening, a couple of my friends and I were going to the hall to see a movie. Edgar came up to us and grabbed me by the arm. He kind of twisted my arm to my back and made me walk outside to his truck. I heard one of my friends saying, "Just like he owns her." It was kind of scary, but I guess it made me feel good in a way. He made me feel wanted, and I liked the idea that he wanted me all to himself. I went out with him on and off throughout that first year, just dating casually. But it got more serious after that.

One night we parked the car down at the beach, down at the bank. People used to go there and park, by the reserve there. I wanted to go home, but he wouldn't listen. We stayed parked there all night. He tried to take off my clothes, to pull off my pants. I was scared and I wanted to run away, but I was more scared of dogs. It was the middle of the night and there were always dogs roaming around. I started crying and he finally left me alone. He was just scaring me, I guess. By the time he drove me home, it was coming daylight.

I got a licking from my papa that time, and I couldn't even speak up for myself. My papa was furious. He said, "I don't want any more bastards around here!" I was really hurt because he believed I had been having sex. I wasn't though, and I wanted to defend myself, but I could never talk back to my papa. I couldn't just say, "No, I'm innocent. I didn't do anything." I didn't talk like that to him, ever. So I didn't say a word or deny anything. I felt dirty the way my papa talked to me that night and helpless because I couldn't find a way to say what really happened.

That whole first year I went out with Edgar we were never intimate. I thought it was because he respected that I wasn't ready yet. Because of that I grew to trust him more. At the time, I really thought I cared for him and that he cared for me. Then one spring evening, my friend and I went to a hockey game or something like that. We got a ride from her boyfriend, and his brother was in the car. There were four of us. At the end of the night, Edgar saw them dropping me off. Edgar often stayed at his sister's house, and he could see out the window to my place. He was a very jealous guy. Right away, he thought I was going out with somebody when he saw me getting out of that car. I wasn't though; it was just my friend's boyfriend dropping me off. But Edgar never believed me.

That night he took me out and he forced himself on me. I was shocked. At first, I thought he was just trying to scare me, like he did the last time. But this time he didn't stop. He raped me. When he was done, he told me that now he had done that to me he would leave me for good. It was just a threat though. He didn't leave me.

I was still in school that time. I remember thinking in class how it really changed me, being intimate with my boyfriend. That was honestly how I thought of what had happened. I didn't really understand that it was rape. I thought it was normal. I suddenly felt out of place there, like I just wasn't the same as those girls anymore. I wanted to tell somebody, but I couldn't. I was so scared because I thought I was pregnant right away. I thought that was how it worked, and I was really scared. It was not long after that, maybe even that month, that I left school for good.

I felt like there was more of a connection after that first time with Edgar. I wanted to see him all the time. I thought I loved him. When he would come down to the reserve he used to just jump out of the truck and grab me and start hugging me and kissing me, just like somebody that's really in love. I believed then that he was. It was very short-lived though.

For the next few months, we were intimate every weekend. Then it happened. I think it was New Year's Eve or New Year's Day when I found out I was pregnant. It was hard for me to tell Edgar. I didn't know how he would react. I told him when my parents and I went to Scanterbury to visit Edgar's family. They said he wasn't home at first. I have a feeling he didn't like it that I went to see him, because I could see how poor they were. They lived in a log house with no electricity or anything like that. I think he was ashamed. But then those old people finally said he was upstairs, so I went up. I told him I was pregnant, and he didn't say anything. I guess he didn't like it.

I was too scared to tell my parents. I was maybe two or three months pregnant already when my mama found out. She asked me, "How come you don't ask me to buy Kotex anymore?" I didn't answer her, but that's how she knew. She didn't say anything right then, but I knew she knew. I ran away because I felt scared of her reaction. My mama always used to say, "If you ever get in trouble, you'll be put in the reform school for girls." I felt so scared of her. I didn't want to go to that school. I'd be sent away to school again, like in a boarding school. That terrified me, and I didn't want to be in a place like that after my experiences in residential school. So when she found out, I took off.

I ran away from home and went to Winnipeg to stay with my sister Rita. Edgar had left his guitar at my house, and I remember I sold it in town for ten bucks. That's what it cost to take the bus to Winnipeg. Somehow, I managed to get to the bus stop in town with my little suitcase. I was so nervous and unsure, riding that bus alone into the city. I can't remember if I phoned my sister and they picked me up at the bus depot, or if I took a cab there and they paid for it. I just remember how scared and alone I felt as the bus made its way down the highway.

It was my first time staying in the big city. I was only sixteen and pregnant. It was scary for me when I first came to my sister's place, but I stayed there for about a month, and it was okay. She lived with her husband and three children in a little house on Lorette Avenue. Rita was a nurse, and I'd babysit during the day while she was working at Grace Hospital. Helping with her kids made me feel less alone.

I wrote Edgar a letter while I was living at Rita's, and before too long, he came to see me. He took me to that log house in Scanterbury to live with him and his family. Shortly after I moved there, the RCMP came and found me. I guess my parents had phoned them when I ran away because they didn't know where I was and were worried. I told the officers that I was pregnant and didn't want to go home. They told me they couldn't really do anything because I was already sixteen, and so it was my choice. I was still too scared to face my parents, and I thought it would be better staying with Edgar and his family. It was tough living there though. Like I said before, they were very poor and there was no electricity. They also weren't very nice people, and I never felt welcome there.

I didn't stay there very long. When I was about four months pregnant, I got very sick. I think I almost had a miscarriage. Edgar's brother Norman and his wife drove me to Pine Falls Hospital, which is about forty-five minutes north of Highway 59. I was admitted and stayed there about a week. From there my parents came to get me, and I went home with them.

All I remember about that drive home was how cold they were towards me, and how scared and alone I felt. Still, I stayed at my parents' place for the rest of my pregnancy. I was still sick for some time after getting out of the hospital, and all I could do was lie in my bed upstairs feeling lonely. I kept drinking lots of water. I craved water all throughout this pregnancy. A week or two after I got home from the hospital, Edgar came to the house asking if he could see me, but my parents wouldn't let him.

Edgar went to the shop and spoke to my papa. He asked him if he could marry me. I heard my papa telling somebody later, "Edgar said to me, 'I love her, and I want to marry her.'" That's what he said. I remember those words because at the time, they meant something to me. That's how it happened. I found him very brave when he went to go and ask my papa to marry me, knowing how they felt about him.

My parents didn't want me to get married because I was so young. I was only sixteen and my parents were strong Catholics. They really believed that once you're married, you're married, and that's that. They didn't want me to get married to someone that wasn't right for me just because I was pregnant. They felt that I was too young to know and didn't want me to be in an unhappy marriage for the rest of my life. Divorce would have been out of the question. They really believed in stuff like that. If they hadn't held those beliefs, I'm not sure they would have stayed together.

My parents were not really affectionate. I only saw my papa hugging my mama once. She was crying because someone had said something mean to her after mass at the church. My papa told her not to cry. He said, "You know it's not true what they're saying. Just forgive them, pray for them. They're doing themselves wrong by talking like that, by saying those things." It was the only time I ever saw him holding her.

I didn't know until after I was much older and my sister told me about some of the things that went on in their lives. My papa wasn't home a lot, and apparently, he would go out and cheat on my mama. Sometimes he'd be gone for a long time and my mama would sell a lot of her sewing to buy food when he was away. I think it was hard on her, but apparently my mama had affairs too. They cheated on each other. Still, I never saw or heard them fight, or even argue.

Not a single physical or verbal fight. As for me, I believe that's a good teaching. It's not good to fight or argue in front of children. Parents are always the best teachers when they live in a good way. Maybe my papa knew never to fight in front of his kids.

They stayed together until the end despite all their problems. My mama and papa used to tell my sister, "When you get married, you have to keep your vows." She had a hard life with her first husband, my sister Virginia. He used to drink a lot, and I used to see her getting beaten up when I was little. I used to just stand there and cry. I remember one time he was beating her up and I grabbed a shoe and started hitting that guy in the back. My sister was just scared I might get beaten up too. I don't remember what happened after that though. Despite my parents' feelings about divorce, eventually she did leave him. After a time, she remarried a man who was much better to her. It couldn't have been easy for her to go against my parents and get divorced. Our parents taught us that you had to keep your vows and stay together. For a long time, I believed that too.

Around the time of my first pregnancy, my biological father returned to Sagkeeng. I can recall seeing him only once as a child before that. I was around eight, and I remember there was something wrong with me. I think I had eczema. He came to the house, and I remember him taking me into his lap and rubbing salve onto my face. His hands were rough and strong, but his touch was gentle. I remember how good it felt to be held by my father like that. He didn't stay long though. That moment is all I have of him from my childhood. By the time he returned for good, I was sixteen. We never became close, but there was at least some connection there.

In time, Edgar managed to convince my parents that his feelings for me were genuine. Before my parents agreed to let Edgar marry me though, my papa talked to my biological father to see if he had anything to say, to see if he agreed or had an objection of some kind. I don't remember what he said, but he probably didn't object to it because they were allowing me to get married, and they were the ones who raised me.

After it was decided that we could get married, Edgar was allowed to come and see me. He was living in Scanterbury, and he would come down to my parents' house and stay with me for a few days here and there. By that time, I was feeling better and was back to working hard around the house. I did all the laundry. I washed floors and washed walls and everything. I even cut wood. I didn't mind because it kept me busy, and besides that, Edgar and I were together a lot throughout my later pregnancy, and I didn't feel so alone anymore.

We planned our wedding. We bought rings and I even had my wedding dress. My dress was really nice. It was a lovely, soft shade of pink and went down to my ankles. There was a zipper on the side. I had a veil too. I had a bridesmaid already. I asked my friend Linda to be my maid of honour. We were originally going to get married before the baby was born, but then we thought we would wait until after.

It was a hot day in August when my son was born. I was tired and I slept through most of the day. I didn't even know I was in labour. I woke up with stomach cramps and my sister-in-law Annie told me, "You're in labour!" I always got along with her. She taught me a lot of things throughout my life. She said, "You better go to the hospital." She called my papa at work, and the next thing I knew, my papa was driving me to the hospital. We went to the Pine Falls Hospital. My papa didn't stay because he was working, so I was alone when my boy was born. My water broke as soon as I got there. I had an easy time when my son was born. I was only in labour for a couple of hours. I remember being taken into the operating room, and then before I knew it, there he was. Just like that. It was so fast. Suddenly I was a mother. I had just turned seventeen.

At that time in Sagkeeng, they used to announce a wedding by ringing the bells each Sunday for three weeks leading up to the marriage ceremony. They call it Pigamiuk in Ojibway, which means "Posting of the Bands." They rang the bells for me and Edgar. We were supposed to get married after Errol was born and everything was ready. In those months before my son was born, I really thought I could be happy. Then everything changed, and we didn't end up getting married in Sagkeeng at all.

Edgar's drinking started getting out of control after Errol was born. One night he went to my brother's house drunk and was trying to start trouble. He and Alec fought. After that, Edgar was mad and took off to drink some more. Something must have triggered him, because after that it was chaos, and he used that fight as an excuse all the time. He was always driving around, drinking, picking up girls, and getting into trouble.

Errol was about three months old when I first suspected that Edgar was being unfaithful. One night he went out with this girl and didn't come home until late. When he finally did, I saw blood on his pants. I wasn't sure, but I had a feeling about it. Not long after that I caught him in the act. I was walking home from the hospital with Errol. I'm not sure what was wrong with him. Errol was often sick when he was a baby. He was always in and out of the hospital. I had walked all the way from town to Edgar's sister Eva's place where we were staying. It was nothing for us to walk in those days though, it was just how we got around. When I got to Eva's place, my son was sleeping. Edgar wasn't home, and Eva said he was watching the ball game by the church. I wanted to go look

for him, so Eva offered to watch Errol. I left him with her
and went to the ballpark to look for Edgar.

When I got there, I saw him in his car with these two girls.
One of them was just getting out when Edgar saw me. The
girl shut the door, and he made kind of a power turn and
took off. I went over to that girl and asked her, "Who's that
in there with him?"

"Oh," she said, "that's Amanda."

I remember how my body felt that time. I felt weak. I felt
sick to my stomach. He didn't come home until late that night.
I questioned him, but I already knew the truth.

"Who was that in the car with you today?" I asked him.

"No one. Just some lady who hired me to go see her
grandpa at Victoria Beach."

I knew he was lying, and he knew that I knew. I had seen
them together in the car and he had seen me. From then on
it was no secret that he always cheated on me. Something
died inside of me that day, and whatever love I might have
felt for him was gone. I had no more illusions that we could
be a happy little family. After that first time, I couldn't have
cared less what he did or who he did it with.

One night, not long after that, he smashed up his car on
the road near where we lived. My parents saw what happened,
and when he came to the door, they could tell he was drunk.
My mama and papa tried to keep him out. He pushed my
mama hard on the chest. She had a bad bruise from it. They
called the police on him, and he went to jail for assault.
I think he got six months, but he was out before then.
My parents didn't want me to marry him after that. They saw
his violence and put a stop to the wedding plans.

I may not have loved Edgar anymore, but things were
getting bad at home, too, and I wanted to get out. There
was drinking, and there was violence all the time. Even
though a lot of people lived there, I felt alone. My brother

Fabian was drinking a lot back then, and I didn't feel safe around him.

This one time he said to me, "You gotta get out of here. You and your bastard."

I didn't have anywhere to go, and I felt really threatened and alone. I didn't feel protected by anyone. Edgar wasn't allowed around there anymore, and I felt my parents couldn't or wouldn't protect me. They were kind of scared of Fabian, too, and besides, my mama still favoured him. I didn't feel safe at all. It was one of the reasons I left.

I felt very alone, and Edgar still wanted to marry me. I didn't want to marry him, but I felt it was my only way out and that I had no other choice. The way I thought was, "I might as well get married. No guy's going to respect me now that I have a child. Besides, where else am I going to go? I don't know the first thing about what to do, how to live, or how to take care of a baby. Who's going to feed me if I leave him?" He was the one that planted those doubts. I was so easily led. Maybe if someone had talked to me, put some sense in my head, I wouldn't have got married. Even at that age I knew how to keep house, to grow food and take care of kids. I knew how to work hard and earn money. I didn't need Edgar. He'd never been involved with caring for Errol, or anything else for that matter, anyway. He wasn't taking care of me. Yet still, that's what I thought. I thought I needed a man, and that Edgar was the only man who would have me. I didn't feel worthy of anything better.

I felt trapped. I was young and I didn't want to be with Edgar anymore. To be honest, when I think about it, I didn't want to be a mother. I knew there would be no happy family with Edgar and that without a baby I would be free to leave. Then, with Errol being sick as often as he was, always in and out of the hospital, it was a lot of work caring for him, and I was doing it all by myself. It was all so hard, and I was so unhappy. I often wondered what would have happened if I hadn't become pregnant.

I spent many years wondering about what might have been. Would I have married Edgar? I knew I didn't love him, and I knew that he was dangerous, but I felt trapped. Then again, I wonder now if I would have become promiscuous if it weren't for Errol coming when he did. It happened that way for so many others who experienced the kind of abuse I did. There are so many "what ifs" in life, and they can really hold you back. The way I see it now is that things happen to you, and you end up with certain people for a reason. I ended up with Edgar. For all the pain it caused me, I learned a lot of lessons, and the experience led me to where I am today. I don't regret becoming a mother. I wish I could have protected my kids and cared for them the way they deserved. But I know that I did the best with what I had, that I love them, and that I will never regret being their mother.

There are times when I think I can't go through with this book. It is painful thinking and talking about the things that I experienced as a kid. I don't know which was worse: my experiences growing up as a child or the horrors I faced later in life. I think that they are equally painful. There are certain energies that kids carry after being victimized. I was taken advantage of over and over again throughout my childhood and well into my adulthood. I felt that my parents didn't care. I think they knew. I believed that my mama knew and just didn't care. I always carried that pain. My childhood experiences made me vulnerable and normalized abuse.

Maybe that's why I put up with so much of the cruelty in my marriage, at least in the beginning. In the end, leaving wasn't a simple matter of standing tall and walking away. To leave meant risking my life and the lives of my children. For eighteen years, I stayed in an abusive marriage, but I survived. I know that the values my parents taught me, as well as the trauma and abuse I endured, gave me the resilience I needed to stay alive and to keep my kids alive through the worst kind of hell imaginable.

This is the reality for many women living in abusive relationships. It is never simple, and it is rarely safe. I'm telling this story for women who might have similar experiences. I want them to read this so they don't have to feel alone. I want to tell them that there are others who can relate to them and understand their pain and recognize their strength and resilience. I want them to know that they can overcome all the pain and abuse and find themselves. So as hard as it is, it's important that I go on and tell my whole story.

4

Mrs. Olson

IN OCTOBER OF 1960 my biological dad got married. It took place on a Saturday in Sagkeeng. I was at the wedding dance when Edgar showed up. I left with him, knowing that if I didn't, he would do something, and the day would be ruined for everyone. I got into his car, and he just started driving. I could tell he had his mind set on something, but he wasn't saying anything. Finally, as we were coming up to Grand Beach, I asked him what was going on.

"Where are we going?"

He looked at me and smiled. Not a soft, loving smile, but a cold smile that seemed to say, "I've got you." Then he said casually, "You wanna get married, don't you?"

I looked straight ahead and said, emotionless, "I guess so."

We slept in the car in the bush somewhere near Bélair that night. The next morning, we drove the rest of the way to Scanterbury. There was an old church near Edgar's parents' place. It's not standing there anymore. It was torn down years ago. It was a little old church. It only had four or five benches and a tiny altar. That's where we got married.

The Father said a mass and married us with just Edgar's dad, his brother Norman, and his youngest sister Diane as witnesses. During the ceremony I was actually grinning.

Somehow, I found the whole thing kind of funny. I don't remember what the priest was saying, but I kept wanting to chuckle, to laugh. I didn't take it seriously at all. I didn't even listen to that priest. When we exchanged the vows, I don't even remember saying, "I do." But in the end, I had a ring on my finger, and I was married. My wedding band was a plain gold wedding band. He didn't have one. I don't know where he bought that wedding band from. They're a lot of money nowadays, but at the time he only paid about ten dollars.

One day, not too long after we were married, I threw that wedding band into the stove when I caught him running around on me again. That ring didn't mean anything, but my small act of defiance did. Maybe it would be easy to label me a victim. But for all of that, there was always something of a fighter in me. I had a spark in me that no amount of abuse or fear could ever fully extinguish. This is just one small example of how I kept it alight and held onto myself.

The night of our wedding, Edgar left for Petersfield, near Selkirk, where he was a guide for American duck hunters. I went back to Sagkeeng with that priest because he had to go there for something, and I had to pick up my son from the hospital. I was nervous to see my parents, and I felt bad for going against their wishes. I knew they didn't want me to marry him, and I was scared about how they might react. It was the Father who told them. I think he knew how scared I was. When he dropped me off, he told my parents, "She's Mrs. Olson now."

My papa was really upset. "She's what?" Then he turned to me and said, "Go pack your bags and get out of here. Don't ever come back."

I quickly put my stuff in boxes. I felt so hurt and alone. The priest took me to my sister Helena's house, and I stayed there. Weegwas lived close to Pine Falls with her husband

and kids. I stayed there until my son was discharged from
the hospital. I don't really remember how long it was or how
I got back to Scanterbury, but once Errol was discharged,
I went to live with Edgar and his family.

When I married him, I really didn't know anything about
Edgar. I was only fourteen when I met him. I always felt
kind of scared of him. From the beginning he intimidated
me, but because of my youth and my circumstances, I was
drawn to him. He wanted me and that made me want him
too. I really didn't know a thing about him. The truth is that
he was a psychopath. He had no conscience, no heart. He
was deeply disturbed.

Years later, after Edgar was gone, I shared a lot with my
counsellor and friend Bernelda. She told me one time, "You
know, Diane, it sounds like he was a psychopath."

I asked her, "Why do you say that?"

She explained how he seemed to have no feeling. He
wasn't educated, yet he was intuitive. I thought it was almost
like he could read my mind. He knew who he could prey on,
and he knew how to do it. He was dangerous.

It took years, but eventually I started to put together the
truth about who this man was. When we first started going
out, he would talk to me, share little things about himself
and his family. Others who knew him would tell me things
too. Eventually, I experienced the worst of it for myself. It
was not until after I left him that I began to understand,
through my own reflections and intensive therapy, how he
became the kind of person he was.

Edgar's family was really poor. They lived in a big log
house, but it was old and very rundown. When I first started
living there in 1960, they had no electricity. There was no
running water, no television, no radio, nothing. It was so
different from my parents' home. It had a veranda with a
roof over it in the front. The house was long and the whole

first floor was open concept. The floors were ugly – just big boards with holes in them. They had old chairs, benches, and a big wooden table with a tablecloth. I remember it had some kind of pattern, flowers, but it was faded, old. Their stove was a big cast iron cookstove that opened on both sides. We had a fire going all the time. That's what they used to heat the big kitchen and cook meals.

They had another stove on the opposite side of the house where the beds were, where Edgar's parents slept. There was a couch there too. Edgar and I shared the little room in the loft upstairs with my sister-in-law Diane. She was about the same age as me. I remember there was a window on each side of the room. The walls were covered with paper and blue dry wash, something like limestone. There were two small cots, smaller than twin beds. They were the same kind of beds they had at the residential school. Small, narrow, old-fashioned, and very uncomfortable. It was just cramped and awful up there.

Most of the time I was alone in that house, or with those old people and their daughter. Edgar was never around. Things might have been hard living in my parents' home, but everything was so much worse when I left. I had no idea just how bad things could get. When I got married, I jumped from the frying pan into the fire.

There was no happiness in that big log house. There was no laughter. At least there had been laughter at my home. There always used to be laughter. But in that old log house? No, it was always full of negativity. Edgar's mom was a very jealous woman, and I think his dad was a womanizer. I used to hear her talking to her husband, accusing him of being with others. Edgar's sister Eva told me that the old lady used to go confront the women as well, swearing in Ojibway. Edgar's dad was Métis or white. He had hazel eyes. He never spoke the language, but she spoke in Ojibway to him anyway.

I think he understood some things, at least the swear words, and he'd have known he was being put down and yelled at.

The old lady looked like a real Indian. She was very dark. Her name was Rosalie, and she was wicked. Rosalie always called people down. The whole family would gossip together about everyone. They'd see somebody walking on the road and say, "That person is sleeping with their daughter," or "Why are they talking like that?" or sometimes, "This one is bad medicine." The old lady was always talking about curses and having bad medicine sent to her. They put a fear into me about the people in Scanterbury, like they were bad. I stayed away from everybody. I lived in a bubble. Years later, when I would go over there on my own, I learned that those people are not at all like that. I was brainwashed, I guess. That's what it was. I was influenced by them and made to feel scared of people and to believe that they were bad. It left me isolated and vulnerable.

I do believe that terrible things happened to Edgar that must have influenced him and made him the way he was. When Edgar was a newborn, something strange happened to him and his brother. Eva was the one who told me this story. She doesn't make up stories, so I believe her. She said that one day worms started crawling all over their clothes. They kept changing them and changing them, but the worms kept coming back. She said they'd clean and hang their clothes, but right away they would be covered in those things. They had them doctored, and only then did those worms go away. They never did find out who was responsible or why that happened to those boys, but there was no doubt that it did happen, and it did affect them.

There was this one woman that Rosalie used to talk about, who I think they believed put that bad medicine on Edgar and his brother. I used to hear Rosalie say things to her old man about Mrs. Pine. She was an Olson before she got married. Rosalie was always saying bad things about her. Edgar himself told me once, "*Those* Olsons were always evil." I guess his family never got along.

Edgar also believed he was cursed by Mrs. Pine. He said, "I went to their house one time with my cousins, and that woman gave me an orange. I knew I shouldn't have eaten that orange, but you know, it was a real treat." They were poor, and fruit was rare for them. So Edgar ate that orange. Later, he believed that it was meant for him. He said that shortly after eating it, his eye started getting small, and it was leaking. His mouth began twisting to one side. Something was happening to him. It lasted for quite some time. Edgar's face was still twisted when he heard a strange rattle in the bush and got lost.

Edgar told me about that time. He was in the bush, and he heard a rattle, right by his feet. He said he kept jumping away from it, but somehow that sound would follow him. He grew up in Scanterbury, and he know the bush around there well. By the time he was twelve he was already good with a .22 and would shoot prairie chickens and other small game. But when that happened, he got lost in that bush – totally got lost. He said it was really weird. Eventually, he saw somebody walking far up ahead, and he went towards them. There, he found a trail that led him to the main road. That's how he found his way back. He said it was bad medicine that got him lost in the bush.

His mom and dad believed it, too, and took him to Ontario to a medicine man, and he was doctored over there. They were told to put an ointment of some kind in four places on his face: the corners of the mouth and one corner of each eye. After that, that thing went away, and his face went back to normal.

Shortly after Edgar was healed, Mrs. Pine saw that his face was better. She told Rosalie, "You think he's better. You think you had your boys doctored. You took them to a medicine man when they were babies and got them doctored. The worms went away, and now Edgar's face is better too. But you're going to see what they're going to be like later on. They're not better at all."

I often wonder about that, after seeing the way that those guys were. Edgar and his brother were both crazy and cruel. I wonder sometimes if bad medicine had a part to play in making Edgar the monster he turned out to be, or maybe the medicine just revealed something that was already there.

Edgar grew up in a miserable, abusive household. There was so much abuse in that family. I know his mother physically and emotionally abused him, but there might have been more. A few years ago, people started to talk about things. They said that old lady was an abuser, that she sexually abused a number of kids in the family. I don't think she ever abused my kids, but I don't honestly know.

I think his dad abused him too. There was no love there. I never noticed a closeness between Edgar and his dad. He was always very angry with him. When Edgar was a kid, his dad used to take him out to isolated places. They'd go to the trapline where he must have been molested. As a counsellor, I heard a lot of stories of abuse happening out on those traplines. Friends of mine who are also in the field of counselling say a lot of child abuse happened on those traplines. That's why I kind of think that maybe it happened to Edgar out there as well.

Years later, one of their relatives told me how when Edgar's dad died, she had a flashback that brought back the feelings she had about him when she was small. "I had a flashback when I saw him in that coffin. When my mom lifted me to kiss him, I suddenly saw myself in my diapers. He was holding me. I remember feeling really uncomfortable and I was crying. I didn't like him. There's something that happened, but I can't remember." She said, "Something not good."

I was also told that his older brother abused him, and although Edgar never told me himself, he did tell some stories that made me wonder if there was something going on there. One time, he told me how he was sharing a room with his brother, and they were making shadow puppets in the moonlight one night. His brother said, "Look, Edgar." And he showed him the shadow of his privates on the wall. He made his privates look like someone dancing. He was laughing about it. Those were the kind of memories Edgar shared with me about growing up in that old log house.

Edgar hated his parents. He used to take advantage of his parents without a thought. When he didn't get his way, he would retaliate. They were scared of him. One time that old man said, "Edgar is very wicked." He told me about a time when he wouldn't lend Edgar the truck. Edgar was mad and he stabbed a hole in the gas tank. It was that kind of behaviour that made them afraid of him. He especially hated his mom. There were times I would hear him yelling at her, "I'll shit in your grave, you fucking bitch." That's how he talked to his mom. He was in prison when his mom died. He never went to the funeral. His siblings tried to get him to come, and he was granted permission, but he wouldn't go.

His mother was very mean to him. His sister Eva talked about that. She said, "I always felt sorry for my little brother. When he was only about two years old, I remember my mother hitting him with a stick and saying, 'Somebody stop me before I kill the little bastard!'" She used to give him real good lickings. He told me how they used to leave him home alone, starving, for two weeks at a time. I saw the way his mom treated him, too, even as an adult. She mistreated my kids, too, just because they were his.

It was because of his mom that Edgar hated his little sister. She favoured her. Eva never told me directly, but she implied that Edgar might have done something to Diane. Then one day Diane opened up to me about what happened. This is just what she told me: She said that she has a memory of being little and falling off a wagon after being pulled down by Edgar. She remembers her private area being full of blood. She said, "Edgar is the one that hurt me."

"He raped you, didn't he?"

"Yeah. That's what happened."

She said, "He hurt me to hurt our mom." He hated her so much for being the favourite, for being babied by their mother. That was how he punished her and got back at his mother.

By the time he was twelve years old, Edgar had become a perpetrator. His sister was not his only victim. One of the kids he abused is in a mental hospital now. She's been there for years. I believe he molested and raped a lot of innocent children. I used to wonder why all the little kids in the family were so scared of Edgar. They didn't like him. They were so scared of him they would go and hide somewhere as soon as they saw him. He must have done something to them too.

His brother was a convicted pedophile. His first wife divorced him after discovering that he was raping his own daughter. He remarried and had more children. He raped them all. He would take pictures of them and had sex orgies with them. Eventually he got ten years in jail for molesting his kids. There was so much hatred in Edgar's family, so much dysfunction. They're all sick. I didn't know any of that about him or his family when I married him. It wasn't until years and years later when he was being investigated that I found out that he molested and raped a lot of other young kids. I didn't know I had married a monster.

This sort of horrific abuse does not get talked about the way it needs to be. The abuse that took place in residential and day schools is starting to be acknowledged, but this is a much more complicated beast. It would be easy to say that all of it can be linked directly back to these schools, but that's not always the case. Colonialism and intergenerational trauma is complicated and brutal. People are afraid to talk about it, so it keeps happening. Maybe they fear that people will think we're all abusers or victims or that all this abuse is because of our culture or some kind of genetic predisposition. All I can do is hope and trust that society has moved beyond those kinds of simplistic and racist ideas. I am openly sharing these stories and experiences because I believe that facing brutal realities can lead to change and healing.

5

Holes in the Walls

I GOT PREGNANT AGAIN about four months after my son was born. I don't remember much of this pregnancy except that I was miserable, and Edgar was away most of the time. He lived a single life. He would be out doing farm work, picking potatoes, or hunting. Always some kind of seasonal work. He never gave me any money, and I heard he had girlfriends all over. I remember always feeling lonely.

Sometimes Edgar would drive his parents to Winnipeg on pension day. The old man had veterans' allowance, so they'd all go to Winnipeg to shop, and the odd time they would bring me. They were heading to the city once when I was about eight months pregnant with my second child. I wanted to go with them and go to Sally Ann and buy some baby clothes. I had five bucks saved up and that was a lot of money for me in those days. Edgar said I couldn't come. He wouldn't take me. I guess because he had girlfriends and would be going to see them. He didn't want me around. They all said there was no room in the car, but there was. They could have taken me.

I remember running after the car, trying to get into the back seat. He stopped the car and jumped out. He just threw me to the ground. I landed on my bum. It was the first time he was really violent with me. I was sitting there crying, and they just drove off. I was really hurt. My feelings were really hurt because I was pregnant, and I was left behind again. I was sore. My back was just so sore that time. I thought I was going to have an early delivery. I didn't know where to go. I didn't really know anybody in Scanterbury, and I couldn't go to my parents. I ended up going to my sister-in-law Annie's place, the one who lived near my parents. She kept asking me how I was feeling and was going to call somebody for help if I needed it. I stayed with her a while. That's all I remember. They came home late that night. He never even said that he was sorry for what he did to me.

Donna, my second oldest, was born a month later in Pine Falls Hospital. Donna was very small for her age. I remember she only weighed five pounds, six ounces. She was tiny. Edgar wasn't there much for any of his kids, but he was affectionate with Errol and Donna when he was around. He'd tease and play with them. He especially seemed to like Donna. He favoured her, but he wasn't really ever there, even for her, and he didn't provide for them at all. I don't even think he was capable of real love.

I was very lonely, and I missed my mama and papa. I was hurt that they kicked me out. I thought I would never see them again, but two years after I left home, they finally sent for me. They told me that they would see me visiting Edgar's sister and missed me. She lived just across the road from them. It always pained me to be so close to home and not be able to see my parents. I didn't think they wanted me, but they said it was hard for them too. My papa was lonesome for me, and they wanted to see their grandchildren. Finally, they sent somebody for me to come and visit.

After that, I was back and forth between Scanterbury and my parent's place in Sagkeeng quite a bit. I tried not to ask for anything. I never bothered my family or told them what

was happening to me. I didn't want anybody to know that
I was being abused, especially my parents. I found out years
later that they knew anyway. My parents used to see Edgar
driving around with different women. He didn't like my
parents because they had stopped the wedding. So he did
this deliberately, just to show them what he could do. My
parents felt bad for me and helped me out a lot in those days.
Still, I was very isolated in Scanterbury, and I really thought
no one knew what I was going through.

There were times when Edgar would leave for months on
end and his parents would kick me out of the house. He was
gone all that summer in '62, fooling around with some girl.
My kids and I were kicked out and had to stay in a little
shack outside of his parents' place. The walls were made of
wooden boards with gaps between them that you could see
right through to the outside. I would use rags, paper bags,
or old newspaper to patch up the holes in the walls so the
mosquitoes wouldn't come in. I don't know where I would
have gotten newspaper from; we never bought the paper.
Maybe I got old ones from the store somehow. Anyway,
inside the shack there was a little heater stove for cooking
and this wooden apple box to keep what little food we had.
We never had much food. I also used the wooden box for a
chair. There was a little homemade table, about two or three
feet high, that was built against the wall. I slept in a small
cot with my two kids. We stayed there nearly all summer,
half starving – and I mean half starving.

When my two little ones and I were living in that awful
shack, I used my family allowance to buy lard. I always made
sure I had lard to make bannock. I would have to steal the
rest of the ingredients from Edgar's parents. Those old
people used to be gone for days sometimes, and when they
were away, I'd go inside their house to steal food for my kids.
I went in through the window. Sometimes they would hide

the food, and then we had to do without. When I could find it though, I would steal some of their flour and rolled oats. I would cook bannock and make porridge for my son and myself. I was still breastfeeding Donna. I did that until she was a year and a half. I had absolutely nothing. I was very skinny. Oh, man. That's what I mean when I say we were half starving. I had a really, really hard, hard life. I was hungry all the time.

It got to the point where we had nothing at all. I was desperate. I got a ride into Winnipeg to look for Edgar. I heard he was staying at his brother's, and sure enough that's where I found him. They were living on Jarvis. Back then the street was crowded with all these old houses. They're not there now. There's new buildings and new housing. My sister-in-law Mary-Ann and her kids were living there too. She told us we could stay with them if we got jobs to bring some money in to pay for our rent and food.

I went out and was able to find a job in a sewing factory that same day. The factory was close by, and I started work right away. I was still breastfeeding Donna though, and she was really attached to me. She wanted me and would be crying all day while I was at work. Edgar stayed home with them when I went to work, but even with him she just screamed.

After only a day or two, Edgar took his car and left for Bélair. It was August, and blueberry picking time. He knew a lot of people in Bélair, and he had a girlfriend there too. Soon after that, I had to quit my job. I was only able to work for five days. No one wanted to babysit for me because my daughter was so hard. I got a little paycheque, but my sister-in-law grabbed all that money right from my hand. I thought she was kind of mean. I didn't even have anything, and she just took it without a second thought. I was used to that kind of thing. Then she said, "You'd better go and look for him. He's in Bélair picking blueberries and probably making money." I guess she figured he would take care of my kids and me.

I asked my friend Sandra and her boyfriend Cole, who were also staying there, if they could drive me out there. Her boyfriend had a car and was from Bélair, so they agreed to take me. She was going to come, but then they got into an argument, and she didn't want to go, so Cole drove me without her. When we got there, Cole knew exactly where to take me, where to find Edgar. There was this area where people were camping in Bélair, and that's where he was staying, spending his time with the girl he was seeing. I recognized his car right away, and that girl was standing outside talking to him. I was carrying Donna when I went over to go and talk to him. I had to ask him for money. I didn't get the chance. As soon as he saw me, he just punched me. Just like that. I went flying onto the sand. I fell hard, holding my baby. I remember feeling really hurt. He tried to fight me right there, but the people standing around us stopped him.

I ran and jumped back into Cole's car. I asked, "Can you drive me to my mama's? Down in Fort Alec?" He agreed, and we took off down the highway. Edgar got into his car and chased us. He was driving really fast, almost hitting the car. I knew he wouldn't stop, and I was afraid we would all be killed if we kept driving. I told Cole, "Pull over."

Edgar got out and came at us. He had a hammer in his hand. He was going to fight that guy. Edgar yelled at me, "Get in the car!" I jumped in the car, my little boy with me and my baby in my arms, of course. That was right on the corner of 11 and 59. Cole turned around and started back towards the city. I thought Edgar would leave Cole alone if I did what he wanted, but he didn't. Edgar got back in the car and chased him again. They were driving really fast. I think he was scared of Edgar. Then Cole lost control and flipped his car. Edgar just went right by without even slowing down. Edgar laughed and laughed. He said, "I hope he's dead."

Later, I heard that he had lived, made it out with only minor injuries. Then, years later, I found out why Edgar was so intent on going after Cole. Apparently, Cole had something going on with the girl Edgar was seeing too. That's why Sandra got mad and wouldn't come with us that day. They were arguing because she knew he would be seeing that girl there, and she knew about them. That's why Edgar and Cole hated each other. They were fighting over that girl. She was very young. She was only about thirteen at the time. Of course, I didn't know about any of this until way after when Sandra told me. She said afterwards that she was sorry that she didn't go with us. She thought maybe Edgar wouldn't have behaved like that if she was there. Later, he accused me of being with Cole too. Maybe it was the fact that I was travelling alone with Cole that made him mad, but you never could tell what would set him off.

Edgar was with that young girl for many years. In those days we'd often be going to or from Fort Alec on Sundays and he would stop in Bélair to see her. I can't remember how many times he would leave me and the kids to wait somewhere in a ditch by the side of road while he was with her. I heard they had two kids together. I don't know if that's true, but I know about one for sure, a boy. He's the same age as my youngest, so she would have had him in '66, about four years after that incident by the road. My kids have a relationship with him and some of Edgar's other kids. He's got seven or eight kids with other women, all from after we were married. He had lots of girlfriends, and he took advantage of a lot of young girls like this one. Like myself.

Occasionally, my kids and I would stay in Sagkeeng for a few days at a time. He'd always leave me there while he was out fooling around. Sometimes we'd stay in a tent outside

his sister Eva's place. I remember sleeping there with my
two kids in the tent, in the summertime. It was nice to be
surrounded by the green grass and the trees. I always really
liked being there with my kids.

One summer when we were camping out there, he came
back in the early morning after being out all night. He had a
girl with him. He told me to come with them and go for a ride.

I said, "I can't just leave these kids here."

"They're sleeping. Come on," he said, irritated.

Of course, I was scared of him already, so I agreed and
got into the car. I hated leaving my kids alone, knowing they
would wake up and be scared to find me gone. They were so
little.

When we came up to Catfish Creek, he pulled over. He
told us both to get out. They started talking together and
I only overheard parts of their conversation.

He said to her, "Okay then, what are you going to do?"
I didn't hear her response, but she kept looking over at me.

"You chickenshit," he said.

"What do you mean I'm chickenshit?" she said, her voice
getting louder, angrier.

It became clear that he wanted that girl to fight me, but
she wouldn't. She didn't have any reason to fight me. I don't
know why he would do that, have me beaten up. Because
she stood up to him, nothing really happened. After a while,
he gave up trying to convince her and dropped me off at
Eva's. My kids were sitting outside the tent, crying. I was
upset, furious really, about the whole thing, but I feared
him. I was glad when he left again right away.

A few years later, when I was pregnant with my third child,
probably about seven months along, I was staying at my
sister-in-law Annie's place. I don't know where Edgar was,
but I was at the hall there when that same girl came and
blew some smoke on my face.

She sneered, "Are you still mad at me over your husband?"
I told her, "You can have him. I don't want him."

"He tells me I'm a hundred percent better than you," she
said, pointing her cigarette at my face.

Then she came really close to me and I just pushed her.
I grabbed her and I just flung her like she was nothing, like
a piece of rag. I remember some guys were saying, "Give it
to her! Give it to her!" They said to me, "She deserves it."

I guess I had enough. Sometimes the way I was being
treated would just get to me, and in that moment the anger
just came streaming out of me. It didn't matter that I was
pregnant. I just went crazy on her, even banging her head
on the stairs.

She was crying and yelling at those guys, "Stop her!
Stop her!"

They said, "The hell with you. You asked for it." I
remember that.

I had a scratch on my nose from that, but the real pain
came later when Edgar fought me for it. She told him that
I said she could have him, that I didn't want him. I paid
for that.

Earlier in that pregnancy we had finally moved out of
his parents' log house. Edgar's brother, Norman, got a new
house, and we moved into the old house he had abandoned.
There was no ceiling, and you could see the frost on the inside
of the roof. It was a very cold house. I kept a fire going all
night. Sometimes I would fall asleep, and I had to restart the
fire. The floors were made of plywood, and I would scrub
them at least once a week. I was glad to be away from Edgar's
parents, but I had a hard life there. I worked hard to survive,
cutting down trees, chopping wood, hauling water from the
river and all of that. We barely had anything to eat. That
winter I was able to buy a bag of potatoes, a bag of porridge,
and a sack of flour. I would make bannock, porridge, and

potatoes, and that was all we ate throughout the entire winter. Lots of times I didn't eat at all, but I made sure my kids ate. That's what you call poor.

One time my sister Helena came out to visit me. I guess she had left her husband by that time, and she came by with her boyfriend. Right away she noticed how skinny I was. "Holy smokes! What the heck are you eating? Why are you so skinny?"

I was very skinny. I hardly ate because I always saved the food for my two little ones, Errol and Donna. We were very poor and there was nothing to eat. I remember when I had the two kids, family allowance was only five dollars per child. So I would get ten bucks a month. It wasn't much, but I'd buy a lot of stuff out of that. I knew how to stretch it as far as it would go. Mainly I would buy lard, flour, baking powder, and a bag of rolled oats for porridge. I made that last a long time. Lots of times we didn't have any sugar, so we would just eat the porridge plain.

Edgar showed me how to use a gun, a .22. I was a pretty good shot. I used to shoot prairie chickens, and I'd cook them for the kids. My family also helped me a lot. I would go there quite often with my kids when we had nothing to eat. Sometimes they would even come to Scanterbury and drop off a box of groceries, all the basic stuff like sugar, flour, tea, baking powder, and lard. That really meant a lot. Most times back then there was hardly anything to eat, and their help meant survival.

The whole time I lived in Scanterbury I was isolated. I was always alone. Edgar was always gone. He stayed on the farms where he worked or with whichever girl he was with at the time. He was always gone either fooling around or in jail. One time he got six months in jail for driving while impaired. Another time he did three months for assault. I guess he fought somebody at the store, and they called the police on him. That was why he was charged for assault. He got six months in jail again, but he was out in three. He did quite a few jail times over the years. Edgar never gave me any money, and I stayed home with the kids. I was lonely all the time, but it was better when he wasn't around.

I managed without him. I worked hard. Sometimes, in the late spring and early summer, I picked medicines like wee-kay by the river. I traded this wee-kay for food and bars of soap for laundry. There was an older couple, maybe in their sixties, that used to buy the medicines from me. I would walk there with my children. It was only about a mile away from where I lived. That lady would make tea and feed us bannock with jam. Those times were always really special to me. I was very grateful for them.

When he was in jail, we could sometimes get welfare and wouldn't be starving. There were no food banks or anything like that at the time, and it was hard to get welfare. During the nine or so years I was living in Scanterbury, I think I got welfare twice. We only got welfare at those times because he was in jail. Most of the time I had to manage by myself. Those were tough times in Scanterbury, but things got worse. Poverty and isolation were only the beginning of my troubles.

During my third pregnancy, Edgar's violence towards me escalated. He came home a few times after drinking and beat me up. I started feeling scared all the time because I never knew what to expect when he got back. One time he even put a knife to my stomach.

He said, "Is that baby mine?" He knew it was his because he knew I never went anywhere. I was alone all the time. Still, he threatened to stab me.

He never apologized for what he said or did. The next day when he was sober, he just said, "I know the baby is mine. I don't know why I feel like this about it." He never treated this child right. Right from the beginning he hated her.

Just across the old road there was a spring with fresh
water flowing all the time. That was where we used to go for
our water. One summer night when I was about three or four
months pregnant, I walked there with my two little children
to get water. As we walked, I saw some people coming towards
us. When they came closer, I recognized that it was Edgar
walking with some girl. He was holding hands with her. When
he saw me, he dropped her hand and came straight for me.
Without a word, he grabbed me and threw me on the ground.
He started kicking me. I could hear my kids crying, but
I couldn't see them. He ripped my blouse off. My sister-
in-law came running and stopped him.

When she pulled him off me, I got up quick and grabbed
my kids. We ran and hid in the bush nearby. My two kids and
I were lying quiet, hoping he wouldn't find us, but somehow,
he knew where we were hiding. He started shooting towards
us with a .22 rifle. I could hear sticks breaking when the
bullets were hitting just above our heads.

He shouted, "Come out of there or next time I'll aim lower!
I know where you are."

Shaking, I stepped out and followed him with my kids.
Our house was just a few yards away. We went there and
he started beating me again. He knew I was pregnant.
I reminded him while he was beating me. He said he
didn't care.

Late in my pregnancy, I used to go picking potatoes at
the farms nearby east Selkirk or Lockport whenever I could.
Throughout the season, there would be a truck that would
pick up workers early in the morning at Gibson's Store at
the crossroads. Sometimes my sister-in-law Diane would come
too. I would pay my mother-in-law a dollar to watch my kids
for the day. Or sometimes my other sister-in-law Mary-Ann
watched my kids for me, but she charged me a dollar fifty.
I would make five to six dollars a day though, so I could still

buy lots with what I had left after paying them. I would buy
a sack of potatoes and eggs from the farmers I worked for.

I remember one time I bought eggs and baloney with the
money I made potato picking. When I fried them up for my
kids, my little girl Donna said, "Mummy, we're rich now, eh?"
That's how she felt eating baloney and eggs.

I heard that Edgar was out potato picking, too, staying at
the farm and spending a lot of time with his girlfriend. I even
overheard people talking about him going to Northmain
Drive-In movies with her. When he was around, he would
sometimes talk openly about his girlfriend with his friend
Derek. He didn't care if I heard what he said. By this time,
I guess I didn't really care anyway. I was numb and too
scared of him to even react to what he was doing.

Edgar happened to be home when I went into labour
around three o'clock that winter morning in 1963. He went
to borrow his parents' car and we left our two other children
with them. My sister-in-law Mary-Ann came in the car with
us because she had delivered babies before. We weren't sure
we would make it to the hospital on time. She kept watching
me and saying, "Hang in there." I was lying in the back seat.
I remember the roads were very icy. It had rained that day,
and everything was freezing in the cold night air. I remember
Mary-Ann took some white flannelette blankets with us,
I guess in case the baby was born in the car.

We made it to the hospital just in time. About ten
minutes after we arrived, my daughter Sharon was born.
She was very tiny, like Donna had been. She was just over
five pounds. Sharon had a darker complexion than her
siblings. I think I was in the hospital about one week, and
I can't remember how I got home. I had baby clothes and a
couple of little quilts I made that I carried in a little suitcase.
I made sure I took these to the hospital with me. Sometimes
I wonder how my daughter was born normal, after all that

happened to me when I was pregnant, but she was perfectly healthy.

Within a week of returning home with my newborn I had to get back to all my usual chores. Back then I was still doing all my washing in the tub with a washboard. My sister-in-law gave me baby laundry soap to use. I hung the clothes outside on the wash line. It was very cold, and there was a lot of snow. I think that's how I got sick. A few days later I was very sick. I couldn't do anything. Edgar went to see this old medicine man that lived a few houses away. This old man came over and made some medicine, which he put in a big one-gallon jar. I had to drink four cups a day until it was gone, and he said that I would feel better in two days. In exactly two days I was one hundred percent better.

After Sharon was born, my sister-in-law gave me a flannelette sheet, which I cut up to make receiving blankets for my newborn. I also kept all the clothes from my other babies that they outgrew. I always managed somehow. We had an old crib somebody gave us. What was really hard was how cold it was in that house. I remember her crying in her crib at night when she was a few months old. She must have been cold.

Edgar couldn't stand it. He would say to me, "You'd better shut her up or I'll kill her."

Even before she was born there was something off about the way he felt about Sharon. After she came, it only got worse. He would say things like, "I know she's my kid, but I don't like her. I don't know why I feel that way about her." It hurt me to hear the way he talked and see the way he treated her through the years, but I didn't know then just how bad things were for Sharon. I didn't know until years later, until it was too late.

I got pregnant again with my fourth child in the fall of 1964. I was still living in Scanterbury, but the kids and I were spending a lot of time in Sagkeeng staying with my parents. One time, we were there when Edgar phoned for me to come back home. My parents drove me back to Scanterbury, but he wasn't there. I don't know where he was, but the house was destroyed. He had broken all the windows. I had my parents leave me there because I was afraid of what he would do if I wasn't there when he got home. They left me with a box of groceries. I put cardboard on the windows to stop the mosquitoes from getting in, like I had when we stayed in that little shack behind his parents' house. When he didn't come home that night though, I went back to Sagkeeng with my kids.

Not long after that, that place was officially condemned. After that we moved back and forth, staying with either his parents or mine. This was a very hard time for me. I felt unwanted in both places and very lonely. My parents had traded the big house I grew up in with my brother Alex because he had so many kids. So they were living in his small, grey two-bedroom house down the road. They still had kids and grandkids living with them though, so there were seventeen people all living there together at the time. It was very cramped and uncomfortable.

Things just kept getting worse and worse with Edgar too. He started questioning and beating me through the nights. I used to dread going to bed; I would dread the coming of the night. When we would go to bed at night, he used to ask me questions about different guys that he thought I went with. If he heard stories about me, he'd question me, and if he thought I was lying he'd whack me across the mouth with his fist. That's why I have a bunch of scars all over and my mouth is not the way it used to look. I used to try and block my head with my arms to protect myself, but then he'd get really mad and yell, "Keep your hands down!"

I couldn't sleep until I knew he was asleep, and I knew I would be safe. That made it really hard because he would come home at all hours. I had to get up early in the morning to look after my kids while he would just stay in bed and sleep through the day. Then he'd be gone until the early hours of the morning when he would come home, and it would start all over again. I'd end up getting a ride to Sagkeeng somehow and go and stay with my parents, just so I could have some rest. Even there though, he'd often come down and we'd go through the same, horrible routine of questioning and beating.

I never cheated on him. Even before I met him, I had never had any boyfriends or dated anybody. It was only ever him. Still, he said I was a whore because I wasn't a virgin when we met. I never told Edgar about any of the abuse I went through as a kid. I didn't really know about all that happened because I had repressed it all. Somehow, he knew though; and as though it was my fault, he made me pay for it. That was his excuse for treating me that way, or one of his excuses anyway. The thing is, all that time I thought I deserved it. I believed that I was bad. When you're told enough times that you're no good or you're a whore, you start to believe those things. I was never good enough.

Edgar was always jealous and possessive, yet he went with all kinds of women like it was nothing. I don't think he ever needed a real reason to accuse and beat me, but I also know that lies were told about me that he used against me. There were two women in particular who really hurt me. Both had affairs with Edgar, and both told lies about me that got me beaten and left for dead. These were women I thought were my friends. When I finally broke free of Edgar it was in large part because of the love, support, and sense of self-worth I gained through genuine friendships with strong women who inspired me, but at that point in my life, I had little self-worth and little understanding of what a real friend was.

One of these supposed friends of mine was a very good-looking girl named Shelly. She told a lie about me that got me beaten nearly to death. Back then, they used to have AA dances in a little building not far from my mama and papa's. So this one time I went to a dance with Fabian, and with Alec and Annie and their two daughters. It was summer and close by, so we just walked over there. I was able to leave the kids with Virginia at my mama and papa's place. She didn't want to go for some reason that time. It was always lots of fun there because we all liked dancing so much.

We were sitting to the side talking when Shelly came over to us. She says to me, "Somebody wants to see you outside."

I said, "Who?" I thought Edgar might have come to get me, so I looked towards the door. This guy I had never seen before kind of poked his head around the door frame.

She pointed and said, "Him."

I had a bad feeling right away. I thought to myself, "What the hell is she trying to do?" "No way," I said to her. I was scared and I didn't go out there to meet him, no way.

Later, when Annie and I went to use the washroom outside, that guy came up to me and grabbed my arm as if to pull me towards him.

I told him, "I'm a married woman." I pulled away and took off.

A few months later we were staying at my parents' place again. One morning, when Edgar got back about six o'clock, he said, "Get the kids ready. We're going to Scanterbury." I sensed that he was very upset. It wasn't the first time he had done this, but something felt different. He did not talk all the way to Scanterbury, which is about a forty-five-minute drive. I was very scared. I knew something was up.

When we got to his parents' place no one was home. I was terrified because of the way he was behaving. He started questioning me, asking if I cheated on him and trying to make me admit who I had sex with. Again, he always did that, but this time it felt different. Edgar said Shelly told him she'd seen me with a guy, that guy from the dance. She told him that she had seen me getting into his car. I didn't even know he had a car. In the end, Edgar made me say that I went with that guy. It was a lie. I don't know why she made up this story. He tortured me for hours. I thought it would never end.

That day, Edgar heated up an iron poker in the wood burning stove. He put it eight inches in, made it just red hot, and he burned me up on the legs. I remember I was screaming and pressed against the bed there, on the wall. You could see a sort of steam as he pressed that poker into my skin and the smell of the burning flesh was sickening. From the look on his face, it was like he was getting enjoyment out of burning me like that. I had five deep burns on my thighs. I still have the scars. I was seven or eight months pregnant when that happened.

I couldn't walk. A couple of days later, a field nurse happened to come by the house for one of my regular prenatal check-ups. Edgar was gone moose hunting with his brother, so I was home alone. I was limping from the wounds on my legs, and I was not able to leave the house, they hurt so badly. The nurse took me to the hospital in Selkirk. They said they were third-degree burns and they were badly infected. The nurse asked me what happened, and I told her, not realizing she would report it to the police.

My three children were with my mother-in-law and my sister-in-law Diane. They didn't know what happened to me. They were keeping my kids because they thought I was just sick from the pregnancy or something. I was supposed to stay in hospital, but I was worried about my children and needed to get home. The nurse agreed to drive me back with my medications, but before she took me home, she made me go to the police station. I had to tell them what happened. They made me admit that it was Edgar who burned me up.

Edgar got back from hunting late that night. The police were waiting to arrest him. I guess they thought they were protecting me, but he was out the next day on bail. His brother Norman went to pick him up. Edgar said they got a good lawyer. He told me his lawyer said, "You know, you can get any guy off the street to say that she's a liar and that they went to bed with her." He said it would be easy to prove I was fooling around on him, and I could lose my kids for being an unfit mother. I believed him and I was very scared, so the charges were dropped. After that he always threatened me that if I ever put him in jail again, I'd be dead.

The other woman who I had thought was my friend, but who turned against me, was Violet. When we were staying in Sagkeeng he would be with her most nights and come home around dawn. He would question me about different guys that she would tell him she had seen me with. He would hit me and question me over and over again, trying to make me admit that I went with someone else. She was the cause of so many of those beatings.

One time I was walking with my daughter, holding my girl's hand, when I saw Violet. Right away I felt the anger flood over me. I was so angry at what this woman did. I thought, "It's not enough that she goes running around with him. Why does she have to lie about me and get me beaten up?" I'm all scarred up. To this day there's still a dark scar on my back where he used a knife on me over some lie she told about me. I thought to myself, "I'm gonna get you if it takes me ten years."

Sometimes I was tough when I was angry, just like when I was a kid and would fight back against those bullies at school. One day I did get back at her. I was at the ballpark. There were beer gardens there and all kinds of stuff going on. I think it was Treaty Days. She was sitting on the ground on a blanket with her auntie and her cousin. I just walked right up to them and I gave her a real good kick in the face, square in the jaw.

It knocked her down and I just let her have it. "You have to lie about me? Tell lies about me? You're sleeping with my husband. It's not enough that you're sleeping with him? You can have him! But you don't have to make up lies about me." I told her, "I got beaten up really bad. Almost got killed because of your mouth."

It felt good to get her back, but it didn't change anything. Even after that, whenever I ran into her, she would say horrible things to me, like, "Hey, Ugly!" and "He calls you ugly." She used to do things like that, in public. She must have felt safe, like Edgar would protect her from me. They always called me ugly, and I believed them. Yet I was a nice-looking girl, a nice-looking woman. I can see that now.

Violet and Shelly were supposed to be my friends. That was what hurt the most. I never understood how either of them could do that to me. I was so hurt by them, and so filled with anger that for the longest time all I could think about was revenge. Edgar had affairs with a lot of women who called themselves my friends. To this day some of them still don't know that I was aware all along that they'd slept with him. I used to hate them even more than I hated the women who flaunted their affairs and treated me like garbage. They continue to act like they care about me, but really, they're two-faced. You don't do that to a friend. But now, I don't hate them. I just don't have respect for them. They don't mean anything to me. In my healing journey I worked through the hatred and learned to forgive. I thought I'd never forgive these women, but I did. Forgiveness doesn't mean allowing hurtful behaviour or being friends with those who have mistreated you, but it does mean letting go of the anger and moving forward. That is what I have done.

My daughter Karen was born in the spring of 1965. My brother-in-law Norman and his wife brought me to Selkirk. Indian Affairs gave me some money just before that, and I remember shopping for baby clothes while I was in labour. I also managed to buy a new blanket and a small gown for my baby to come home in. I was by myself for her birth. I was happy when she was born. I cried because I was so excited, but I was also lonely. I phoned my parents collect to tell them I had a little girl, and I talked to my papa. Karen was very fair and had light hair. I breastfed all my kids except my first-born, Errol.

I got pregnant again a couple of months after Karen was born. So then I had a son, three daughters, and another child on the way. Edgar was in and out of jail throughout this pregnancy and had an affair going on, the same young girl he was with when Donna was a baby. She used to write letters to him, and in 1966 she got pregnant too.

I was in Scanterbury most of the time, staying in the old log house again. His parents had abandoned it by then, so it was just me and the kids for the most part. His parents lived nearby with their daughter Diane. She now had two children with her boyfriend, who was living there too. Their house was quite nice. We used to go over when we were really hungry and had nothing to eat.

When I was about two months pregnant with my youngest, I went to see the chief of the reserve and asked if I could get a house. He said, "I'll try, but you have to come up with $150 for a down payment." I told my parents about it and asked them if they could help me out. They saved up

the money for me to put down on the house. I couldn't
have done it without them. I went to the band office and
told them I had the money. I also went to the Indian agent's
office in Selkirk. The agent's name was Mr. Daggit. I told
him I had been staying in an abandoned house for the last
six years and that we were desperate for a new house. I also
asked the Indian agent if I could get help to buy clothes
for the baby I had on the way. I was already showing by
then. Edgar was in jail at the time, and I remember so well
what Mr. Daggit said when I went to him. He said, "I'll
help you out, but not him." I knew even then that Edgar
had a very bad reputation. He was always in and out of
jail. But it really sunk in when he said that. I was grateful
because a lot of the time no one would help me because
I was with Edgar.

We were approved for the house, but of course we couldn't
expect to get it right away. So we had to make do in that old
log house through the winter. The old log house still had no
electricity or running water. That winter, and even into March
and April, there was a lot of snow. I had to go out into the
bush to cut trees with an axe for firewood. I'd haul these trees
on my shoulders, walking through snow up to my knees and
sometimes to my thighs. I would cut the wood to fit the
cookstove to keep my kids warm and to cook our food.
I worked hard during all my pregnancies.

I was cutting wood when the chief informed me that
I would be getting a new house by the next year. I was so
happy. He also said he would get someone to bring a load of
firewood, and he even gave me a twenty-five-dollar voucher
for food. As soon as he'd gone, I took that voucher straight
to Gibson's Store just down the road. I had just walked into
the store when I went into labour. It's a good thing my sister-
in-law Diane and my mother-in-law were around. They kept
the kids while I was in the hospital.

My son Randy was born in the evening. He was very fair skinned, with blondish curly hair and hazel eyes, which changed to brown when he was about eight months old. He was exactly seven pounds at birth. I was in labour for twelve hours. He was healthy. It is amazing, actually, that all my babies were born healthy despite all the abuse and poverty I experienced during my pregnancies. I did everything I could to keep them safe. I never smoked cigarettes or drank alcohol during any of my pregnancies. Still, there were so many things that were out of my control that could have harmed them.

I was alone when I gave birth to my children, but I was still happy when each of them was born. After I had my fifth child though, I started using birth control. Then, about six or seven years later, I had a tubal ligation so I couldn't have any more babies. Edgar was hardly ever around and didn't seem to care much for his family. He could be affectionate with Donna, and with Errol too. He favoured them over the others. He would tease them and play with them when he was around. He would tease my youngest daughter Karen, and Randy, too, sometimes, but he never liked Sharon. He wasn't good to her at all.

Edgar rarely took me and the kids anywhere, and when he did, I think he was embarrassed by us. One time, I don't know where we went, but they were crying in the car. "Shh!" He spoke so harshly. He never really took us anywhere. He never took us to baseball or hockey games, or anything like that. The only thing we ever did as a family was pick sugar beets or blueberries.

I guess those were the good times. My kids talk about those things. They used to like when we would go blueberry picking. It was one of the few places Edgar actually took us. We'd have fun. We would make bannock and take a lunch of tea and baloney sandwiches. After picking the berries we'd go to Stead, to sell them and give the kids ice cream, as a treat. I'm glad they have those memories.

We used to make money all kinds of different ways. We would pick blueberries in Bélair and sugar beets around Altona. We would harvest rice in the fall and pick Seneca root by the sandhills of Gull Lake. When we picked sugar beets, I stayed out there with my kids. We would hoe the beets really early in the morning before it got really hot and then go out again in the evening when it got a bit cooler. I could make about one hundred dollars a day when things went well selling those beets.

In the spring we used to hunt muskrats. In the fall it was squirrels. I used to skin those things and put them on a stretcher I made myself. They would dry like that, and we'd sell them. I remember one time we made two hundred dollars. That was a lot of money in those days. Edgar also did a lot of deer hunting then and he'd make money selling what he got.

The issue was never that we couldn't earn money. The issue was that Edgar took all the money we earned for himself. While I struggled to feed our kids, Edgar lived well on the money we earned. I remember Edgar had a nice blue and white vehicle at one time. He bought it one summer in a private sale on one of the farms we were working on. There's actually a picture of me sitting on this car, though of course I never really got to use it.

Edgar basically left us with nothing to live on. I was resourceful though. I kept my kids fed and clothed. A lot of times people would give me hand-me-downs for myself and my kids. One time I got a nice coat from my mama. I don't know where she got it, but I really appreciated that coat. It was warm. When I was able to get welfare, I could buy clothes we needed too. Shoes especially, for my kids. Never new, but I could find nice ones in second-hand stores. There weren't many second-hand stores then, but I used to go to the ones in Selkirk or Winnipeg when Edgar and his parents let me come into the city with them. Sometimes I'd get a garbage bag of clothes for like two dollars, and I'd sew and alter the clothes for the kids. When they were babies, I'd use the money I got to buy ten yards of flannelette from The Bay and make a dozen diapers. I would also make sheets and pillows out of flour sacks I saved.

I had to do laundry nearly every day, especially with all the diapers. I even remember the laundry soaps I used were always either Oxydol or Sunlight bar soap. I don't even think they make these soaps anymore. I'd haul the water from the river, which wasn't far from where we lived, while my kids were sleeping. I used a tub and washboard. That's how I washed clothes.

I used the same tub for bathing my children. My adult children laugh about that today. They talk about having baths in this tub when they were little. My son would go first, and then his two sisters together at the same time. When I had the five children, I would change the water after them, then bathe the two youngest ones. They all enjoyed that. I didn't let on that I was sad living alone all the time looking after my children. I was always busy with them.

In 1968 I moved into my first house that I could call my own. I was determined to make that house nice for my kids. I wanted them to have a real home for once. I went to work for a Jewish family on a farm nearby just so that I could buy furniture. I bought an old bed and a dresser from them, and I bought a stove too. One of the first things I did when I got that house was go to Lockport Appliances and pick out a brand new wringer washer and a sewing machine.

They delivered them to my house. Oh, it was so nice to have a wringer washer. I'm a clean person, and always keeping my kids clean and washing everything by hand was so much work. The sewing machine, too, made such a difference. I would remake second-hand clothes for my kids, and I made blankets too. I'd get old coats from my mama in Sagkeeng, and I'd take them apart and cut blocks and make blankets.

The payments for the washer and sewing machine were ten or fifteen dollars a month. I made payments with my kids' allowance money. For a while I still had enough money left over to buy some food, but pretty soon I couldn't keep up with the payments. The allowance I was getting then was only five or six dollars per child, and I had to buy food. Edgar was out of jail and taking money from me too, so there just wasn't enough.

Within a few months those guys came to take my stuff away. I was at the sewing machine when they came to repossess my washer and sewing machine. I think they felt sorry for me or something, seeing me working hard with all my little children around me.

The one guy said, "I guess you really need that one, eh?" He pointed towards the sewing machine. After a minute or two of talking they said, "We'll let you keep it."

I was so thankful! But I couldn't help asking him, "Can you give me that washer too?"

They both looked genuinely sorry, but the guy said, "No, I'm sorry, we can't."

"Well, can you take the sewing machine instead? Never mind the sewing machine, but leave the washer?"

Again, looking sorry but firm, he said, "No." He explained that the washer was more expensive, and they really couldn't get away with letting that one go.

So I was back using tub and washboard for all the laundry. But I was still thankful I had that sewing machine. I kept it for years and years. I gave it to my oldest daughter about twenty years ago. She used it for a long time as well, but I think she lost it in a house fire a few years ago.

All I wanted was to make a nice home for my kids. I wanted them to be safe and comfortable. I wanted them to come home and have a nice meal cooked for them every day. It rarely happened. I lived in Scanterbury for nine years, always struggling just to put food in my kids' mouths and clothes on their backs. I felt displaced and unwanted wherever I went. I was afraid of my husband and afraid to leave him. I had nowhere to go. I wanted to make our new home nice. I wanted it to be safe.

6

Breakdown

EDGAR WAS CHARGED for murder in 1969. I think it was late spring, early summer, and we were still living in Scanterbury. Edgar had taken the old station wagon that my brother Fabian had given me and gone to Winnipeg. He was supposed to be looking for a job with his friend Derek.

He came back when it was still dark, maybe about three o'clock in the morning. I switched on the light when he came in. He yelled, "Turn that off!" Before I did, I could see that his face was puffed up and bruised. He had a big black eye and he looked scared. He grabbed me and he pushed me towards the picture window.

"See if there's anybody coming down the road," he said. Of course, I obeyed right away, but I didn't see anything. He told me, "Get your shoes on and come with me." I didn't want to leave the kids alone. Errol was only nine and Randy, my youngest, just three. They were all still asleep. I tried to say something, but Edgar didn't care, so I did what I was told.

We walked down the road in the dark. Edgar pointed towards the crossroads. He said, "I left the car over there. Come with me."

As we walked towards the crossroads, I saw my white station wagon in the dark. Then, as we got closer, I could see guys standing around there.

"Holy hell. Holy fuck," he said. They were detectives. They didn't have their lights on, but they had guns. They saw Edgar before he could run. They grabbed and handcuffed him right away.

One of the detectives was standing next to my car with a rifle pointed at me. "Don't come any closer," he said to me. I froze. I didn't know what the heck was going on.

The detectives told me to stand a few feet away, but I could still hear everything. Derek was in the back seat of the police car with Edgar. I heard him saying in Ojibway, "That guy died, you know. Boy, Edgar. That guy died. He died." The detectives wouldn't have understood the language, but I did. That's when I knew he had done something really serious.

Before they drove off Edgar shouted at me to go see his brother Norman right away and tell him to get a lawyer. I walked straight over there as fast as I could. I woke Norman up and told him what happened before I went running home. My kids were alone, and I was worried about them. They were still asleep when I got home. I don't know how I got the keys, but later that day I picked up the car from the crossroads.

Over the next few weeks Edgar's brother Norman went running around to make bail for him. It was quite a bit of money. They really made it high. I think it was something like fifty thousand dollars. The whole thing was published in the paper. People thought he'd never get out. It took some time, but he did. His brother was the one that went around and made it happen. He could really talk. In addition to the bail money, he had to have five signatures for Edgar to be released. He got them all. I remember some important people signed that thing.

While all this was going on I couldn't stay in Scanterbury. There was nothing there for me. There was no food, and I was scared of how people would react to what he did. I didn't want to be there by myself. So, while Edgar was in jail and Norman was running around trying to make bail for him, I took my kids, and I went to my mama and papa's house. I left my home and everything in it when I left for Sagkeeng.

A few days later, I went back with some people from Sagkeeng to pick up some clothes and things like that. Somebody had ransacked our house. All our things were smashed. It was completely damaged inside the house. They poured paint all over the walls and on the little bit of furniture I had. We lost just about everything. The band eventually fixed up that house and gave it to somebody else. The house I had traded with my in-laws was torn down. They tore it down to make sure we wouldn't go back. I guess the community didn't want Edgar back on the reserve. It didn't matter. I didn't want to go and live there anyway. It wasn't a good place for me.

I found out years later, when I was a counsellor at Native Addictions in Winnipeg, that Mrs. Pine was responsible for the damage done to my house. I was told that she hired people to vandalize that house. It was her relative that Edgar had murdered. She must have wanted to punish Edgar. She was in band council for many years, and that was why my kids and I were never able to get help from Scanterbury after that.

Edgar was out that summer. He came to live with me and the kids in Sagkeeng where we were staying at my mama and papa's house. That was when the trouble really started. After that he didn't give a damn what he did. He kept asking me, "Are you going to wait for me? What if I go to jail for two years? How about ten years?" He kept questioning me every night, bringing up the past and asking whether I would wait for him or not. Of course, I said that I would. Sometimes I almost said that I wouldn't because I felt that's what he expected me to say. There was no right answer with him, and every wrong answer was met with violence. Life became even more unbearable.

Rumours can be dangerous things. Terrible things have happened to me because of lies people told about me. Edgar would use lies and rumours as an excuse to hurt me. The year he was charged with murder, Brent Chevres, a guy from Sagkeeng, told people he'd slept with me. Apparently, Brent was telling people he'd "had" me a couple of times, and it got back to Edgar. He must have known it wasn't true, but that didn't matter. Edgar was already questioning me and beating me up whenever there were rumours about me being unfaithful or if he suspected something. For some reason though, this was different. This was worse.

At night I would always lay with my kids in their bedroom until Edgar got back, usually just before daylight. One night Edgar came home and woke me up. There was nothing unusual in that. I left the kids sleeping in their beds and went downstairs with him. There was someone there, someone I didn't know. He had brought home this man with him, and he was waiting down there for us. I didn't know what to make of it and I was really scared.

Edgar said to me, "I want you to sleep with that guy. Go and have sex with him." I was horrified. I had never been with anyone else and didn't understand how he could want me to do that. It felt like a trap. He said, "Well, if it was Brent, you'd sleep with him."

I almost talked to Brent about that. I wanted to ask him, "Why the hell did you say that about me?" You know? "Look what happened to me because of your stupid lies!" I just couldn't understand why he would do that. I almost confronted him, but I was so timid; I was so scared. I couldn't speak up for myself. Edgar was sick, and I'm sure he would have found a way to hurt me no matter what, but it's impossible not to wonder, "What if he didn't have that excuse? Could things have been different?"

That night was like a nightmare. Edgar gave me a bottle of beer. He said, "Drink it fast."

At first, I refused, but he insisted. He said it would be easier for me if I had a drink. I didn't have a choice. I drank the beer. I always did what he told me. There was a mattress on the floor downstairs, and he told that guy he could have me on it. That's where he made me go with him. He forced me to have sex with that guy.

I almost went crazy, I think. After it was over, I completely lost control. As soon as they had gone, I grabbed a gun and got into the car. I was going to shoot up that Liquor Commission where they sold all the booze back then. I was going to go there and just start shooting. I knew how to use a gun. I was going to do it. But before I even pulled out of the driveway, I had changed my mind. It was the idea of my kids growing up without me that snapped me back into reality. I thought, "I'm going to go to jail, and my kids will be all alone if I do this." I pulled out of the driveway and drove straight to the hospital.

I guess I had a nervous breakdown. I had blackouts. One minute I was in the car driving, and the next thing I knew I was lying in the hospital, and they were giving me needles. They gave me needles in both arms just to calm me down. They always had someone there to watch me. I can remember the nurses sitting with me while I lay in that hospital bed and cried.

I think it was the second night in the hospital that I had this dream. I dreamt of the house where we were living. It was dark in there and people were lighting candles. I dreamt that my daughter Donna was in a coffin. I left the hospital the next day because I knew something was wrong. Still,

I stopped at the store before going home because I wanted to bring food home for my kids. While I was there a phone call came for me. Mr. Peru, who owned the store, got the call. He said to me, "You have to go home right away."

My daughter Donna had been electrocuted. She had grabbed a bare wire. She thought it was a skipping rope. Edgar was there when it happened. She was stuck on that wire. I'm not sure how he did it without being electrocuted too, but he said he just grabbed that wire and unplugged it from the wall. She was unconscious. She almost fell in the water when it happened. They said she would have died if she had.

We drove over to the hospital. Edgar was yelling at me. He was holding Donna and I was driving. Fabian was there, too, and he was mad. He said to Edgar, "What did you call her for? You know she just got out of the hospital. She's not well. We could have taken Donna ourselves." They kept her overnight at the hospital. It was a close call.

My dream was like a premonition, and yet I couldn't protect my daughter. I might have been able to stop what happened to Donna if I had been home when I had that dream, but I couldn't be there for her because of Edgar and what he did to me. It wouldn't be the first time I wasn't there for my kids because of him. It also wasn't the last time I would have a premonition. You have to pay attention to your dreams and your instincts. Although in this instance I couldn't change the outcome despite sensing the danger, there would come a time when my instincts would save my life.

After that summer we moved again. Things got bad with my family, and I think we got kicked out. Somebody loaned us a house at the town site where we stayed through the fall. Edgar was out on bail until he went to court in November. He had two lawyers from Winnipeg. They were tough lawyers. I guess legal aid must have paid for it, or maybe Norman, because we couldn't have afforded them on our own. Norman was the one who found the lawyers anyway. His brother supported him so much.

I am sure Edgar murdered that guy. He stabbed him to death at the Manwin Hotel. I have no doubt that Edgar was guilty. In the end though, they didn't have enough evidence to convict him. They never found the weapon. I remember them searching the CN yards. That's where he told them he threw that knife. But you know where that knife was? I found out years later. He threw it in the gas tank. He opened the gas tank, and he threw that knife in there. It was in our station wagon the whole time. I know he killed him.

I also know that this wasn't the first time. When we were living in Fort Alec, he used to go out drinking with this woman and two guy friends all the time. He came home early one morning after a night of drinking with them. It was already daylight.

He came home and told me, "Go and look at the car. See if there's blood anywhere, or if it's dented. I think I ran over a deer."

At the time I believed him. But then, not too long after that, I saw something that made me wonder. I saw him throwing a watch into the river by where we lived. A week or so later, I heard that someone got killed in a hit and run in Pine Falls. His watch was missing.

Edgar had always hated that guy. It was hard to understand his reasons for hating someone. I think in this case it was over a girl. This guy who was killed was a good-looking guy, and he was going out with this girl from the reserve who was very pretty and who Edgar liked. I really think that's all it would take to make Edgar kill.

Years later, when I was already separated from him, I heard something from my sister-in-law Annie that confirmed my suspicions. The woman who Edgar was out drinking with that night told Annie, "I know who ran over that guy, but I can never tell because he's going to kill my kids." She took it to her grave.

"I think that was Edgar," my sister-in-law told me. "Because I seen him drinking with them that time." I knew she was right.

The others who were with him kept quiet too. People really feared him because of the rage he carried. I understand that now today. That's why I say he's a psychopath. Why do you think I feared him so much? Why he was able to control me all those years? He was evil and I was terrified of him. He was a murderer who would kill again. But he wouldn't kill me, and he wouldn't kill my kids. We would break free. One day we would know what it feels like to be safe.

7

Scars

WE MOVED TO WINNIPEG in 1970, after the trial was all over. My sister helped us find a place to live. She was living on Aberdeen in the downstairs apartment of a duplex, and she told me that the two-bedroom suite upstairs was coming up for rent. It had one big bedroom and a smaller bedroom. We got on welfare, and I took a job doing housework so we could afford the rent and have food to eat. We lived in that upstairs apartment for a year before my sister bought a house and moved out. Then we took over her bigger place downstairs.

Being in the city, Edgar started drinking even more and was going to parties all the time. He had so many affairs. During that first year in the city Edgar was having an affair with his cousin's wife. One night they came in while I was sleeping. He grabbed me by the hair and pulled me out of bed, throwing me on the floor.

He told me, "Get the fuck out."

Then he went to bed with his girlfriend there. I had just bought that bedroom set with my kids' income tax money. I was so mad. I couldn't have anything. I took a lot of crap, let me tell you. It was like he had the right to everything, just like he couldn't do wrong. I couldn't say boo. I wasn't

even supposed to get mad. Over the years, things only
got worse.

There are some nights now when I'm lying in my bed,
my nice, comfortable bed, and I think, "Life is good. Life is
grand." I don't have much, but I make sure I'm comfortable
and I know I'm safe. I can do that now. In the life I had
before I had no control and no comfort. I couldn't even sleep
when I wanted to. I could never sleep in peace. I'd never
know when something was going to happen. He'd come home
and if I was sleeping, he'd spill water on my face or hit me
hard with something. He'd wake me up to question me, to
beat me, or to make me go with other men.

He used to force me to leave the house in the middle
of the night and he'd drive us down the highway towards
Sagkeeng. Sometimes we stopped at this camp, along
Highway 59. It was up on a hill. I think they were planting
trees or doing construction or something. There was a bunch
of guys living there. Edgar would make me drink beer and
act sleazy to tempt those guys. I would just pretend that
I was drunk though, because I hated drinking. I remember
everything. They would take turns on me, one after the other.
I had to pretend I wanted it so he could get his kicks. He
was really twisted.

I came to expect it. When he would make me get in the
car at night, I knew what was coming. I hated it, but he
forced me to go every time. Once I tried to get away, and I
wound up in the hospital. We were at a New Year's party way
up on Burrows, close to Keewatin. My cousin lived there.
Edgar was just drinking lots. I had a few drinks, but mostly
I was pretending to drink, because I knew I had to drive,
and I wanted to get home alive for my kids.

After Edgar lost his driver's licence for impaired driving,
I used to have to drive him everywhere. Edgar was the one who

taught me how to drive. He was controlling. A perfectionist. Things had to be done his way. He would hit me while I was driving, and I was always nervous. If I put on the signal to turn, he would hit me for doing it without his permission. I was like a robot by the end. I was afraid to make a move, waiting for him to tell me to put on the signal. Then he would hit me for not putting the signal on sooner. He'd be yelling at me all the time. I was a nervous wreck.

The night of that New Year's party we left at about two o'clock in the morning. He was very drunk, and I was driving, hoping to make it home safely. I was slowing down to turn onto our street when he punched me in the head.

"Go right through."

I knew what was coming. I knew where he wanted me to go, and I just couldn't. I took a right at Selkirk and Main and stopped at the red light.

"I said to go right through." His voice was thick with anger.

I jumped out. Our home wasn't far from there, so I just ran for it. I knew I wouldn't be safe, but all I could think of was that I had to get away. Minutes later, he was there. He came through the back door. He came straight for me. I gave him a kick as soon as he came close, but of course he overpowered me. He started fighting and punching me. He was beating me, and I was screaming and crying. It woke up my kids and they all came running down the stairs.

He was choking me when they came in. Donna wasn't scared of him at all.

"Dad!" she yelled. "You fucking bastard!"

She jumped on him, but he threw her down. I remember her on the floor. He was going to step on her throat. I made a dash for him, and I pushed him away from her. As terrified as I was, I tried to protect my daughter. We all ganged up on him and he left. He didn't come back until the next morning. My left eye swelled completely shut right away where he hit me, and I was badly cut. It would become yet another scar. I paint my eyebrows to hide all the scars he left on me. By morning I was hurting all over, and I could barely open either eye. I would have got it worse if it wasn't for my kids. I don't know how many times they might have saved my life.

Edgar always had a knife, and he kept it sharp. He always had guns and hunting knives around. My kids and I just thought about our safety, that's all. One time he took me to a party at my sister's place on Atlantic. A fight broke out, and he pulled a knife on someone. He was drunk and he was just swinging that knife wildly. He didn't even see where he was stabbing, and the person he was fighting overpowered him. Edgar grabbed me and we ran out of that party. He was mad and acting crazy. I didn't want to go home with him. I was scared because he was going nuts. He threw me on the back seat and told me not to move, but I was terrified and desperate to get away. We got to a stop light, and I tried to open the car door. He reached over and stabbed my thigh. The knife went in deep. I kept trying hard to move away from his knife, but he got me again. This time he stabbed me in the back. The stabbing there was not too deep, but it was enough to stop me then.

I almost lost my leg that time. I couldn't go to the hospital until the next day. It got infected and I had a hard time walking. They wanted to admit me and keep me on an IV for a few days. They said I would probably lose my leg if I didn't do that, but I couldn't. I couldn't stay in the hospital because I was worried about my kids. I went home, but I had to keep the IV in and go to the hospital every day for a strong antibiotic. One day, Edgar ripped that needle out. I waited until he left, then I went to the hospital. My daughter took me. We walked from where we lived on

Aberdeen to the Health Sciences Centre. I've still got scars on my legs from that. That's why I don't wear shorts.

Edgar got some kind of sick pleasure out of watching me with other men. There was this guy who lived in a cabin somewhere around Bélair that Edgar would make me have sex with. One time he took me there and that guy wasn't home. We went into the cabin anyway. Edgar was mad that he wasn't home. That guy had a German shepherd, and Edgar got it into his head that he could make me have sex with it instead. Edgar told me to get my clothes off and go on my hands and knees. He tried to get that dog to go to me. He rubbed something on my private area so that dog would come to me. I was praying that that dog wouldn't do anything. I was terrified. In the end, he couldn't make the dog do it. So because that dog wouldn't go to me, he started kicking me and beating me.

He said, "If you really wanted that dog to come to you, you would make it come to you." Then, he raped me. He used something, I think it was a stick. It was very painful. After that, he pulled me up by the hair. I was standing and he was choking me to the point where I passed out. I don't know how long I was out for. When I woke up, I was cold and naked, terrified, and badly hurt. I could see outside the window. It was dark in the bushes, and there were no other houses around. I remember thinking I should run through the bush, even naked, and try to find someone, to get help. I got up the courage and tried to run, but he caught me and started kicking me again. I was all bruised up. I could barely move the next day.

Recently, I was driving by Memorial Boulevard, and I recognized the old building where the Abbott Clinic used to be. Seeing it brought back those horrifying memories. That was where I was sent to see a specialist for vaginal repair after what he did to me that night. I never told the doctor what happened because I was scared that the cops would pick him up and he would kill me for putting him away.

We all went through hell living with Edgar, but it was probably my girl Sharon who suffered the most. I didn't realize just how much until she was eleven and ran away from home. It happened while I was in the hospital for the vaginal repair surgery. She came to me, with her jacket torn and all distressed. She had run away from Edgar. I asked her what happened, but she wouldn't say. I kept questioning her, asking her why she ran away and why her jacket was torn. I knew something terrible must have happened. It took her a long time before she could speak.

"Why did you run away?" I asked her again and again.

Finally, she responded, her voice quiet but defiant. "'Cuz he tried to do that again."

"What again? Who?"

"Edgar," she said.

"What happened?" I demanded.

"You know."

"No, I don't know," I said. "What happened?" But a horrifying understanding started to creep over me. Oh man, you can't know how I felt in that moment. I said, "Did he do something to you?"

She just burst out crying. Finally, she let it all out. "He grabbed me. He wanted me to take my clothes off. He tried to give me ten dollars to take off my pants. I was screaming and he let me go." After that, she shared everything with me. He had raped her. He had been abusing her for years. It started when she was only four years old. He was molesting her the whole time and I didn't know.

I asked her, "How come you never told me?"

"'Cuz he said that you knew and you didn't care." That's what perpetrators do. I know that now from my training.

They usually tell their victims, "She knows, she doesn't care." But I hadn't known, and I did care. I knew what it was to be abused, even though I hadn't faced it or dealt with any of that yet. I still knew the pain.

That's when I took her out of the home. I placed her with my cousin for her own protection. I explained to her that I was putting her over there for her safety, so that he would never touch her again. I told her, "I wish I could get rid of him, but you know he's going to kill us all if I leave." I told her that I loved her. It was her that I loved, not him. I don't think she ever really understood or believed me though.

Shortly after she left, Edgar tried to bribe her to come home. He offered to buy her a bike. He told her that she could come home, and that she'd be okay. I was in the car when he was talking to her. I made silent gestures and mouthed the word, "No." She didn't come home. She refused. I'm so glad that she didn't come home, even though I missed her. She never lived with us again.

By that time, he had already started making me sell myself. He had me well trained by then. I was so scared of him all the time. He knew what to do, how to control me. He used my kids to make me do what he wanted. He said that if I didn't do what he told me to do I would never see them again. I honestly believed he would take them from me or that he would kill us. I had to obey him.

He started by introducing me to Main Street almost as soon as we moved to the city. The first time he took me out was to the Mount Royal Hotel. I thought it was supposed to be like a date, a night on the town. It wasn't like that though. Everything he did was calculated. He controlled me through fear, and by then I knew to just do whatever I was told. He bought me a beer. I didn't really like drinking, but I did what I was told and drank with him. I looked around and I noticed two ladies kissing and necking each other. I didn't really know anything about lesbians or gay people back then. I had never seen anything like that.

I told him, "Look, those two ladies are kissing."

He said, "That's what this place is about." And he pointed out to me that some of the women in the bar were actually men dressed as women. They had miniskirts, high heels, and lots of makeup on. There were also a lot of young women that were very pretty and dressed nice. He told me those were hookers, ladies who go with men for money. I had never even heard of that. I was still quite naive those days. He knew what he was doing. He was slowly introducing me to Main Street and the life he wanted me to lead. I had no idea what lay in store for me.

The first time it happened we were still living on Aberdeen. Our place was close to Merchants Hotel on Main where he used to take me sometimes. By then I knew what those kinds of places were all about. He came home late that night and woke me up. He told me to go get him a case of beer, but he didn't give me any money. He told me that I would have to find someone to go to bed with me for that beer. I knew I had to do it.

By this time, I already knew how to behave, how to act to make men think I wanted them, because of what he was already making me do. I went out that night, scared but resigned, and I found a guy. I went with him in a car, and he gave me a case of beer for what I did. Then he dropped me off close to where I lived. That's how it began.

It was hard in the beginning, but Edgar knew exactly what to do, how to groom me. He even got me to do Kegel exercises so that the customers would like me. He would always have me drink before making me go out so that I would be more willing. I started drinking more and more because it was easier to do the things I was forced to do.

I didn't care so much when I was drinking. Edgar was perverted. He was completely twisted. He used to tell me to bring my tricks to our house. He told me to bring them there and have sex with them so he could watch. He drilled a hole about the size of a loonie into the floor right above the couch where he had me take the men. He'd watch us through the hole. He got his kicks out of that. At first, he only made me go on the streets occasionally, but before long it became almost every night. Somehow you just get used to it after a while.

When I was on the streets, I used yellow jackets or bennies. Truck drivers use them to stay awake on the road. I would get them from the doctor because I couldn't sleep. I had to stay awake to work on the streets at night. Then I would have to go to work the next day too. When I could get away, I would go hide somewhere in my car or go to my sister Helena's to sleep because I was so tired. Even then I had to use something to help me sleep because I never felt safe enough to really rest.

I was always working. I cleaned houses during the day and worked on the streets at night. Edgar took everything. I was like his slave. I kept and hid what money I could without him finding out. I'd hide it until I had one hundred dollars, and then I'd pay my cousin with it to keep Sharon. Then I would start saving again. I sent one hundred dollars every two weeks until Sharon got caught stealing with her cousin and Children's Aid got involved. They started paying my cousin to keep her after that.

In 1973 Edgar's dad was killed on that new Highway 59 they were building through Scanterbury. Edgar's family got a big pay-out from Nelson River Construction, and his mom started receiving a widow's pension cheque every month. Edgar bought a car with that. His mom would always give money to him, but never with a good heart. She'd just throw it at him and make sure that people saw that she gave him money. She wasn't like that with her other kids. She had a special hatred for Edgar. He hated her too. They were always full of anger and hatred. It was the one thing they had in common with each other.

The same year that his dad died, we moved to the low rental housing development on Stella Walk. Nothing changed. Edgar always found a reason to get mad. There was always something. Everything had to be done exactly the way he wanted, and you could never really tell what that was. I spent eighteen years walking on eggshells. I thought I would never get away. I thought the only way was to kill him, or to end my own life. I hated him. I wanted him dead. I used to pray that he would get killed. I would imagine him in car accidents or being beaten to death or something so that we'd be free from him. Many times, when he was passed out, I thought about how easy it would be to kill him. Once he even said to me, "If you killed me, you'd probably get away with it." He was well known to the cops, and they probably never would have charged me, though I didn't know that at the time. I was always too afraid of what he would do to me if I tried and failed.

Still, if you get pushed too hard you can go temporarily insane. I know because it happened to me. It happened to me more than once. One time, Edgar came home drunk. It was sometime in the afternoon and I was cooking. Sure enough, he found something to get mad at again. I don't even know what it was. I was at the stove, and he just came up behind me and hit me across the back of the head with a big ashtray. I could feel the warm blood dripping down my back. I grabbed a towel and I put it around my head, and right away it was just soaked in blood. I could feel myself getting faint, so I quickly shut off the stove and sat on a chair. I thought I was going to pass out.

I was sitting there trying to wipe myself when he came back into the room a moment later. He was holding a rifle. I remember that rifle was a .30 M1. He made it like a machine gun. He started loading it, looking at me all the while. Then he held the gun out towards me and said, "Here. Come and shoot me."

It happened in a split moment. I went for it. I grabbed that gun, and I pulled the trigger. I was just inches from his head. I could have killed him, but he was fast. He grabbed that gun from me, and he emptied all those bullets. I could have killed him, and he knew it. He hit me over the head again, this time with the stock of the gun, and he left me there to die.

When I woke up there was a pool of blood around my head. I was alone. He was gone and my kids were all out of the house. I got a towel and cleaned myself up as best I could. I even cleaned up the floor a little bit. I didn't want my kids to see all that blood and be scared. I think Donna came home and called a cab to take me to the hospital. I remember my welfare covered the cab. She came with me. She was always the one to go with me to the hospital.

I needed twenty-one stitches across the back of my head. There's a big scar and a dent on my head from that big ashtray. After that, even after the wound had healed, I'd get dizzy if I got up too fast because of that blow on my head. I had to be kind of careful. When Edgar started pushing me around again after I was back from the hospital, my daughter would tell him to stop. Donna was the only one he would listen to.

It was during that time in the hospital that I first heard about Al-Anon. The nurse at the hospital told me that I should go to a meeting, that it could help me. I remember thinking to myself, "Why should I go to a meeting? He's the problem. He's the one that needs a meeting." That was my thinking.

I wasn't ready to get help, but it was an opening. An introduction to the idea that there was help out there. It's important for people in roles like that to know that even if the help you offer isn't accepted in that moment, it can provide a glimmer of hope to someone in a hopeless situation. Eventually, each attempt to reach out, each offering of help or even just a kind word, adds up and can lead to change. So it's important not to give up on people.

I was always so scared of him. It came to the point where I actually came to look forward to going into the street, rather than taking the abuse at home. I was away from him. He was very, very abusive, and so it was easier on the street. I met a lot of good people out there. People that are lonely will pay lots of money just to be close to someone. There was one guy who took a liking to me, and he became my friend. He stopped being my trick after he got to know me and what was going on with me.

He would say to me, "What are you doing here? The guy that's doing this to you should be hung by the balls."

"Agh." I'd just brush him off. I said all kinds of things. I played tough, eh. You become tough sometimes. It was a way of protecting myself. He never gave up on me though. Even when I put him down, he would tell me, "I think you're a good person." I didn't let him know it then, but those words meant a lot to me.

I remember one time, sometime around 1976, I had the flu bad, and Edgar's fourteen-year-old niece was visiting. Edgar was out drinking as usual. I could never sleep when he was out because he would get mad if I wasn't there to open the door when he got home. Or, if I left it unlocked, he would say, "Who are you waiting for?" Either way he would beat me up. So I always tried to be awake when he got home. That night he came home from the bar around two o'clock in the morning.

He said to me, "Let's go to Calgary."

"What? What about the kids? We can't leave them."

He said that his niece could stay with them. Then he said, "Get ready. We're going now." He handed me twenty-five bucks and said, "Give her this to buy food so they have enough 'til we're gonna get back." I gave her the money to buy them food. Then I quickly grabbed my jacket and that was it. That was all I had time for.

We got to Calgary the next day. He made me drive all the way. We got there and still he had me driving all over the city. We were looking for one of his girlfriends that he used to go out with when he was young. He knew that she was in Calgary and would be out drinking because she was a big drinker. He wanted to find her and be with her.

When evening came, he started going into all the bars, looking for her. He didn't let me go in with him. He told me to go work on the street and get him some money. I couldn't do it. I hadn't slept, I was on my moon-time, and I was really sick.

When I told him that he just said, "Use your fucking mouth then."

I said, "I can't. I'm too sick." He didn't care. He wanted a certain amount of money, and that was all there was to it.

So I went into a bar, and I drank a beer, so I'd be brave. It was stupid of me to do, but I was scared, and I hoped I would be able to do what he wanted. I drank maybe two beers and that was enough to get me drunk. I went out into the street, and I was just freezing. It was cold. Before long I gave up and went into the car to lie down. I was so cold and tired. Luckily, I had the spare keys. I was shivering and I felt so sick. I remember I was just so sick.

He was really mad when he came out of the bar, because he couldn't find his girlfriend anywhere and I hadn't made any money for him. He fought me and then we left.

"You're fucking driving," he said.

There was a storm, and the roads were terrible. We almost got into an accident when a bus passed us because he was hitting me while I was driving. We drove late into the night. Finally, I saw a motel up ahead, and I thought, "Oh, I hope he lets me stop."

He did. He said, "Pull over here." We got a hotel room, but exhausted as I was, I couldn't rest until I knew he was asleep. I thought he'd come and fight me again if I did. Finally, he fell asleep, so I could too. The next morning, I drove again. My head was splitting. I was so sick and hardly had any sleep. We pulled over in Brandon and he went to Champs Chicken. He got three-piece dinner for himself and nothing for me. I thought he was so, so cruel.

He saw me watching him as he ate. "You wish," he said as he waved that chicken under my nose. "You wish." It was like he was enjoying that, trying to torture me. I was hungry, but I survived. I was hungry a lot of times. It didn't matter.

I was still the one driving as we continued. I don't know what got him mad again, but suddenly, he reached over and hit me real hard with a beer bottle. It just smashed. All I could feel was something warm dripping. At first, I thought it was beer, but then I touched my head and realized it was my blood. I had a deep cut on my forehead, near my eye. I had to keep wiping the blood from my face so I could see the road. Each time I did he would hit me again and say, "Stop wiping yourself! Just drive."

Before long, my eye was closing from the swelling. I had a hard time driving. I don't know where we were when he finally said, "Pull over." He took over driving then. I thought I might finally get to rest, but as I was falling asleep in the passenger's seat, he hit me. Every time I would drift off, he would hit me hard. He wouldn't let me fall asleep.

When I got home, our kids, my two youngest ones, were sitting on the steps waiting. They ran to the car and grabbed me. They were so happy to see me. Years later they told me about that time when we were gone.

They said, "Not knowing when you were going to come home was torture to us."

They said they had knelt by the bed and prayed that I would come back alive. We shared the same fears. That's why I used to pray too. Each time I thought I was going to die I would pray to survive so that I could go back home and see them. I didn't want my kids to grow up without their mother.

They were all so scared of him. I remember one time I was boiling potatoes, making supper for my kids. I had boiled the potatoes and was draining the water when he came home. He took the pot of potatoes and spilled them over my head. He was so cruel. I was never able to be a good mom and make a home for my kids. I just wanted to be at home taking care of my kids, keeping the house nice and clean and cooking good meals for them. He disrupted everything. We were never at peace.

I wanted so much for my kids to have a good life. My oldest boy was a good hockey player. He was good, but he never had a chance. His dad was never there to support him. He never even bought him hockey equipment or anything like that. I used to pick up things in the second-hand store, or people would give me stuff for him. I remember my friend Stanley had sons who played with Errol. One time his wife told me I needed to buy Errol knee and elbow pads. I guess Stanley told his wife to ask me to buy some stuff for my son. But I couldn't really afford anything because Edgar always took all the money.

My youngest son played hockey, too, but in Winnipeg. It was the same thing with him. I was always struggling, trying to get him the equipment he needed and be there when I could. Edgar couldn't have cared less and never went to his games. Whenever I could make it to a game, he was so happy, my son. I think we all craved normalcy and it was so rare. Most of the time I couldn't be there for my kids because I was always either doing something for Edgar or recovering from one of his attacks. My life revolved around him.

That's why I can relate to these movies: *The Burning Bed* and *Life with Billy*. *Life with Billy* is based on a true story of a woman named Jane who suffered horrific abuse at the hand of her husband. In that movie, the boy said, "Mom, we're just like robots." That's exactly how I felt. I felt like a robot, just going through the motions of life, without ever really living it. In the end, Jane kills her husband. So does the woman from the other movie, *The Burning Bed*. That could have happened to me, too; I came close to that breaking point more than once. My story is different though. I found another way out of that life because of my kids. I believe that sharing how I got out can help pave the pathway for others. It is not easy, but it can be done. I did it.

8

Breaking Free

THE FIRST TIME I tried to leave him was in 1972. It was not long after we had moved to Winnipeg and things were getting worse and worse. Around that time, he spent a lot of the time at his girlfriend's place drinking, so one day when he was gone, I just packed a little bag and I hitchhiked to my friend's place in Rivers. I stayed away for about a week, but all that time my kids were all alone, looking after themselves. I was so worried about them and lonesome for them. I couldn't abandon them like that. So I went home.

Not long after that I took my kids with me and ran away to Osborne House for the first time. Osborne House was a shelter for women and children, which shut down in 2014. I'm not sure how I heard of it, but I think someone from the hospital gave me the information after I came in with some injury from Edgar. Over the years, we ran away and stayed at Osborne House six or seven times. I kept giving up and going back home though. I was sure he would find me, and I feared what he would do if I didn't go back. He didn't love me, but I was his meal ticket, and I knew he would never leave me alone.

Throughout those difficult years, my older children, Donna, Sharon, and Errol, were rarely at home with us. They were in and out of group homes or would stay with their cousins most of the time. I usually just had my two youngest with me when I would run away. There were always a lot of women and children at Osborne House. It was a busy place, but I always felt alone. The workers there said I was very withdrawn. I never really got any counselling or talked to anyone about what I was going through. I didn't see the point in talking.

The people at Osborne House helped me get a restraining order, but it didn't help. One day I was going to a doctor's appointment with my kids. We took a cab from Osborne House, and as we were driving, we ran into Edgar on the corner of Broadway and Sherbrook. He saw us in the cab, and he blocked it with his car. I jumped out of the cab and went running into a Salisbury House that was there then. I said, "Call the police! I got a restraining order!" Nobody listened to me. They just stared and watched as he came in and grabbed me. He twisted my arm behind my back and forced me out of the restaurant. He threw me in his car. My kids followed, screaming and crying. He took us home and beat me up again, of course. Nothing ever changed.

The last time I stayed at Osborne House was in 1978. When you get phone calls at shelters like that, they don't let the person calling know you're there. They don't tell the person anything or allow them to speak to you. They say, "I'll give her a message if she's here." That's what they have to do to keep the people in the shelter safe. One day there was a message for me at the office to call my cousin.

When I called her back my cousin was panicked. She said, "He knows where you are. He's going to shoot up that place. You'd better get out of there." I was so scared that I called him right away and asked him to come and pick me up.

He said, "You're fucking lucky." He said, "I was going to shoot up that place."

It was true what my cousin told me. He would have done it. He would have killed me, my kids, and everybody else there. I didn't tell them why I called him, why I broke the rules and apparently let him know where we were. I didn't even try to explain. They believed that by calling him I was putting myself and everyone else at the shelter in danger. So they never wanted me back there again. I had nowhere to go, nowhere to run now. There was nowhere else to go.

One night, shortly after that, I was in bed, sick. When he came home, he handcuffed me to the bed and said, "You're not going anywhere ever again." He was mad because I had left and now that I was back, I was too sick to go out in the street. He said, "You're no fucking good to me."

My youngest children were sleeping upstairs. Karen was only twelve, and Randy would have been eleven. They were on the third floor, which was a sort of loft. That's where they were sleeping. They didn't hear me yelling and screaming for help throughout the night. They didn't know anything until it was all over the next morning. I am grateful for that. I never let them know what I went through that night. I tried to protect them. While he was beating me, he kept threatening to burn the house down. "Please don't," I begged him. "The kids are upstairs. They're sleeping." Maybe that's why he didn't do it. Maybe there was some humanity in him.

He finally left sometime near dawn. He was living with another woman at the time, and he just left me cuffed to the bed like that and went home to her. I thought, "How am I going to get out of here?" I was handcuffed to the bed, sick and bleeding. He probably forgot about me because he was so drunk. Or he was waiting that long on purpose, to torture me. In any case, it wasn't until hours later that he did come back. He took the handcuffs off. He must have just left again after that. I don't know how I got there, but I ended up in the emergency room again. I nearly bled to death. They kept me there for two days. Once again, I should have been there longer, but I signed myself out because I was worried about my kids.

I became suicidal. I thought death might be the only way I would ever get away from him. I had tried to kill myself many times before, but I had never really meant it. I wanted to live, to be there for my kids. There had always been a little bit of hope keeping me alive, but by then it became serious. I was desperate. I planned how I was going to do away with myself, how to make sure that I'd be gone for good before somebody could find me. I planned exactly what I was going to do. I figured, "I can't be a mum. I can't be with my kids anyway. My mother was gone, and I lived. They'll survive." I honestly thought they would be better off without me. I got some booze and some pills and took them all at once. I ended up at St. Boniface. I was there for two weeks. They put me in Psychiatry and gave me a thorough assessment. I almost died there; I wanted to die, but I guess I just wasn't meant to.

A few days into my hospital stay, Edgar came there with Karen and Randy. He came in there with my two babies and said, "Look what you're doing to your kids." He put it all on me. He made me feel that it was all my fault that they were hurting. He made it seem as though I was abandoning them because I was selfish and didn't love them enough. I already felt that I had failed as a mother. I feared they would never forgive me, but I was wrong. They understood me better than I could have imagined.

Years later, Karen shared with me how she felt then. She said, "I just hated him for that. He was blaming you for being in that hospital. I just hated him." She said, "We both hated him." I know that my children blamed me for a lot of things, and so when she said that I felt so grateful to know that they understood my pain and desperation in that moment.

Of course, that day in the hospital I had no idea how they felt about me, and my sense of hopelessness and guilt consumed me for a long time. All I knew was that if I couldn't kill myself, I would have to find another way to escape.

I thought I found the solution when I was charged for soliciting not long after that. This other girl and I were charged by undercover cops for working the streets, and I was put on probation. The idea of going to jail was not scary to me anymore. I felt that my kids were better off without me, and I couldn't take care of them or keep them safe anyway. If I were in jail Edgar wouldn't be able to reach me. I would be safe and could rest.

I figured it wouldn't be too hard to get sent to jail. I was on probation and was used to breaking the law by then. Throughout those years I used to steal nice, expensive clothes from stores. We called it boosting. People would buy these stolen items from us. It didn't matter where they came from. I guess they didn't think about it. One time I made about eleven hundred dollars when I went to Sagkeeng. Edgar took all that money and before long he was driving a brand new vehicle like a big shot while my kids and I suffered in poverty. I decided that I would get myself caught boosting. That would be my escape.

I remember the day I got myself caught. I had talked back to Edgar about something or other, and I knew I was in for it if I had to go home that night. I had to try something. I wanted to get caught and I did. I had hoped they'd put me into custody right away, but they just gave me a piece of paper to go to court. I had to go home and face him. Thankfully he didn't beat me up that time. He was drunk and threatened me, but nothing serious happened.

I went to court soon after that. By then something else had happened, and I was scared again. I just wanted to go to jail so I could rest my bones and just be at peace away from

Edgar for a while. I figured my kids could go to Children's
Aid. They would be safer there anyway. I remember going to
the courthouse. I told Randy and Karen to wait in the hallway.
They were eleven and twelve. I went in and found my lawyer.
I whispered in his ear, "I want to go through with this today.
I want to plead guilty. I'll just go to jail. Call Children's Aid.
My kids are in the hallway."

He told me to sit down, and he called security to go watch
my kids. I remember that. Then he kind of interrupted the
court in session and spoke with the judge, telling him what
I had said.

"We will put her in custody for a pre-sentence report," the
judge said. So my kids had to be put somewhere. They called
my cousin, who picked up Randy and Karen and kept them
for the five days I was held for. Donna, Sharon, and Errol
were all in group homes then, so they were able to stay where
they were.

Throughout that week, they investigated me and my
family. When the court day came, I stood before the judge
with my lawyer, a court advocate, and Alvin Toll. Alvin was a
probation officer who was already involved with me and my
kids and was a huge support. They all knew about a lot of the
stuff Edgar was doing, and I think they sympathized with me.
I remember the judge telling me, "You can straighten out
your life. I'm giving you this chance. I really believe that you
don't belong in jail. Your husband is the one who should be
in jail." They all agreed with that.

I had to see my probation officer once a week after that.
Alvin knew all about my life. He was a smart and kind man.
He would often do home visits and talk to my kids. They were
in trouble with the law, too, and really needed the guidance.

"You know," he told my kids once, "your mom is a very
strong woman. Any other woman I've worked with would
have left you a long time ago, the way you guys behave and

treat her." It was true that they were very disrespectful towards me then, but I don't blame them. With the way it was at home it was only to be expected. I didn't know how to treat them with respect either.

I was at rock bottom, and he knew it. He told me, "Diane, you need to make a change. He's very destructive to the family." He told me about Al-Anon. He said it was a spiritual program that promotes healing and awareness for people like me.

He said, "You might as well just lay down and die if you don't try this, Diane. You're going to die. You have to do this." I'll never forget that. I had heard of Al-Anon before but had always shrugged it off. Now I knew he was right. I needed something, and here was an opportunity. I had to accept it.

Alvin gave me the phone number for Al-Anon's central office. "Call this number," he said. I did what he said. They knew I was Native, so they connected me with this other Native woman, Bernelda Wheeler. I phoned her and we talked for a long time, though I didn't tell her too much in that first phone call. You don't really have to tell people in Al-Anon your troubles for them to understand. They know. They've been there too.

At the time I felt completely hopeless. I had this idea that I could try to run away to BC. I was trying to find a way to escape, and I wanted to get as far away as possible. I had thought of this before, when I was staying at Osborne House, but had always been too afraid to say anything. It turns out that it might have been a possibility. Shelters can actually transfer families to shelters in other provinces. Sometimes that distance can provide a certain level of protection in cases like mine. I didn't know that at the time though. As it was, I don't think it would have been right for me anyway.

It was Bernelda who helped me see that. She didn't give me advice, she just listened, and then she asked me, "Will leaving change things for you, Diane?"

I had never thought about things like that until she asked me. Just running away had never worked in the past and never would. I would never feel safe or free and would just continue to live in constant fear. I wouldn't be able to raise my kids on the run any better than I was able to raise them at home. After thinking about it I finally said, "No."

I was so traumatized, so messed up from everything that happened. Running away wouldn't have changed that. I had to face it and work through it if I was ever going to be truly free of him. Something happened during that first phone call. Talking with her gave me hope. I was able to start believing that maybe I could find another way. She told me when the next meeting was and offered to pick me up. "No," I said, "I'll go there myself." I was finally ready to take a chance.

The theme of that first meeting was "Courage." There were a few Native women there, including Bernelda, who I met in person for the first time that evening. These women were instrumental in guiding me towards a new life. Years later, Bernelda described her first impression of me. She said I looked so small and scared when I walked into that meeting. In those days, I always had my head down and wore shades to hide my bruises and cuts. I was bruised up most of the time. I didn't want to be seen. I had very low self-esteem.

Everybody shared something with the group. When it came to my turn all I could say was, "It took a lot of courage for me to come here." My voice was flat, and I spoke very low.

A woman named Vera was sitting next to me. She kind of put her hand on my knee, and patting it gently, she said, "I'll be thinking of you. I hope you come back. You need this." That meeting really gave me a lot of hope. These people cared for me.

Talking to Bernelda and going to that meeting changed my life, but not overnight. Soon after, I moved to a house on Warsaw Avenue with my two youngest. I was trying desperately to separate from Edgar, but I was still terrified of him, and he continued to control me. Even though I had moved out and started attending meetings regularly, I was still working on the street, making money for him. It took me a while before I could see that I did have a choice, but I needed to gather the strength and courage before I could make it. Al-Anon was just the first step.

In one of those early meetings, somebody gave me the book *One Day at a Time in Al-Anon* to read, and I hung onto that for dear life. I would keep it hidden and read it over and over again. Edgar found it one time, and he must have read some of it when he did. He yelled at me, "This fucking thing is brainwashing you." Then he threw it across the hall. I was so happy he didn't destroy it, but by then I knew I could just get another one if he did. I was already getting stronger. Once it began, it didn't take too long.

After the Al-Anon meetings I used to go visit Bernelda. I wanted to be like her. I would see the way she was with her kids, and the way they were with her. They treated her with so much respect, and they were so kind to one another. It wasn't like that at my home. I had so much anger, no patience, no parenting skills, and I was constantly yelling at my kids. Despite that and everything else that was happening at home, I didn't understand why my kids wouldn't listen to me and why they had no respect for me.

I soon realized I made a lot of mistakes raising my children. My focus had never been on them because I was always just trying to survive from one moment to the next. So there was not really any discipline in our home. There couldn't be. We were living in constant fear, and I was never free to parent them. I had no idea how to show respect towards myself or towards them, so how could I expect them to respect me?

They were angry with me for staying with their dad for all those years, blaming me for all the violence and trauma they experienced and hurting from the neglect. When I started paying attention to their needs and disciplining them, they were confused. By this time, they were already teenagers and had never experienced this kind of parenting before. My children had a lot of mixed feelings during that time of transition. Some were still rebellious, but they saw that I was getting better and began to feel safer.

I wanted what Bernelda had. I hung out with her a lot. I went to her place all the time, and often on the weekends I would spend nights there. We'd talk and she would listen. She was very understanding and knowledgeable. I wanted to be like her, not only in how she raised her kids, but in how she lived her whole life and gave herself to others. She was a very good counsellor and friend. She was my role model.

I met a lot of good people through her, like my other sponsor, Marie. I became close to Marie as well. We were good friends. I used to go to her home, too, and I always felt welcome. Over the years Marie encouraged me a lot. She listened to me without judgment, never criticizing my children's father or telling me to leave. She knew how important it was that I be able to make decisions on my own now. Sometimes I would take my two youngest kids to visit her, especially Randy, who was always with me. I felt comfortable in her home, and I felt that we could relate to each other. She had six kids, and I learned a lot from her about motherhood.

Bernelda, Marie, and Vera were all strong supports in my healing journey. I got a lot of encouragement and strength from these women. Because of them, I gained the courage to stand up for myself and get another restraining order. I had very little faith in restraining orders, because of my past experience, but I was willing to try again. It was very hard in those days. The police didn't come right away for domestic abuse calls, if they came at all. Today, there's zero tolerance for domestic violence, but back then things were different. There were times the cops would drive by when I was getting beaten up. All Edgar had to say was, "She's my wife." And they would drive away. They would just drive by, just leave me like that.

He breached those restraining orders all the time though. They didn't mean anything to him. He didn't respect the law. One day, shortly after we moved away, he followed my kids home from school and found out where we were living on Warsaw. After that he would come and terrorize us constantly. Scary as it was, Al-Anon taught me that I had to trust that the restraining order would help; that it was worth it. I think it was more about taking a stand and gaining some sense of control and empowerment than anything else.

I really tried to make a home for my kids. That year, I tried to give my kids a special Christmas. I even managed to put up a tree and lights. Of course, he came and ruined everything. He came in yelling and knocked the tree down. The kids all took off to where my oldest daughter was staying, somewhere not far from there. They ran out with no shoes on, just socks. It was really cold. Randy couldn't get out fast enough though, and Edgar caught him. He used my baby to torture me. Randy was forced to watch me get beaten up so many times. He had to watch his dad because he was my baby and Edgar knew it would hurt me. I know my youngest son still has a lot of rage because of that. He's seen so much.

It didn't take long before Edgar completely trashed our house on Warsaw Avenue, and we had to move again. I got a house on Flora Avenue from Kinew Housing. That was in 1979. I lived there with my two youngest, and my older kids used to come around quite often. Edgar didn't stay there but he knew where I was and would come there to collect the money from me. I was still going on the street to make money for him, but I was becoming stronger and stronger, and eventually I gained enough courage to make that change too. It was hard, but eventually I stopped giving money to Edgar and could finally stop going out on the street.

He didn't let me go just like that though. He came to the house one day, looking for money. He had a high-powered rifle on him and was ready to use it. He was mad because I wouldn't give him money anymore. That was what triggered him. He got everyone there to line up and told us, "Shut up and don't make a noise." He didn't want to hear us pleading for our lives as he lined us up to kill us.

He said, "Which one first?" The rifle pointing at us, his finger on the trigger.

My youngest daughter's friend Vicky was there. She went right up to Edgar, kneeling and hugging his legs. She begged him, "Edgar, don't kill your kids! Don't kill your kids!" I think she saved us that time. She was only twelve or thirteen years old. She saved our lives.

Instead of shooting us then and there, he went downstairs in the basement and started shooting up my new washer and dryer, filling them with holes. After that, I guess he was so drunk that he kind of fell on the floor and passed out.

I told my kids, "Get the guns." Edgar had guns and lots of ammunition hidden throughout the house. The kids went and got guns from the basement and started running out of the house with them. We were trying to get them away from there before he woke up. My car was parked in the back. They all grabbed the guns and were throwing them into my car through the open windows. He woke up and he grabbed a gun from one of the kids, but they got away and we ran.

The kids and I jumped into the car. I was just hysterical as we took off. I drove blindly. I didn't know where I was going. I went down Osborne, down Jubilee; I drove on top of a barrier and went the wrong way on a one-way street. I drove to the police station on Jubilee, at Pembina Highway there. We went running into the station in a panic. I said, "He's got a gun! He's got a gun! He's trying to kill us!" I was just freaking out because he was going to shoot my kids. He was going to shoot us all.

Errol, his friend Rick, and my daughter Sharon were left at the house in the panic. Rick was a white kid who came from a troubled family too. I guess they were sitting there in the back room there, even after all that had happened; they were just sitting there the three of them. They didn't care. They had that attitude, like they didn't care if they lived or died.

Later they told me that after we got away, Edgar aimed the gun at Errol, who was sitting against one of the beds. He was going to shoot him, but Rick ran in there. "No!" he said. "Shoot me."

Edgar turned the gun on him and fired. I guess it just missed him by inches. When he fired, he made a hole in the wall, and that plaster sort of exploded, and a fine dusting of white powder went all over Rick's face. It was in his eyebrows and eyelashes. They were all white and when he blinked, he said it fell like snow. They were laughing about it, those damn crazy kids. They said that they were scared, but afterwards they laughed about it. Years later when we were talking about that day, I asked my daughter how it made her feel. She said, "I didn't care if he killed me."

Police cars surrounded the place, and they arrested him. For all the good it did. He was out on bail the next day and came straight back to terrorize us. I was in the kitchen and had just finished cooking some soup and bannock for the kids when he came. Sharon and my two sons were home, just upstairs. He started banging on the door. I didn't get to the door soon enough. Before I could do anything, he took an axe to that door and hit it over and over again until it was in shreds. Then he came in yelling and smashing everything in sight and beating on me. He threw our soup and bannock in the garbage and threw me on top of the table. The table broke.

My son Errol heard all the ruckus and came running down. He was sixteen at the time. Edgar yelled at him, "Get the hell out!" Errol ran out of the room, but he didn't leave. I could see him looking through the crack in the door.

The table Edgar had thrown me onto had heavy legs – stainless steel, or chrome. Edgar took one of the legs and started beating me with it. He caught me a few times on my back, and I couldn't breathe. When Errol saw his dad hitting me with that thing, he came running in there.

"What the hell are you doing there?" Edgar yelled at him.

As terrified as he was of his dad, Errol went right in front of him and yelled, "Leave her alone!" Then, when Edgar started hitting me with that thing again, he pushed his dad.

I saw Errol raise his fists. He was going to fight his dad. Suddenly Edgar stopped and looked around as if he didn't know where he was. Years later, Errol described what happened. He said, "It was like he woke up, but he was pretending." Edgar was pretending that he was coming out of a blackout, as if he hadn't been aware that he was beating me half to death. He couldn't fool anyone. He knew what he was doing.

After that though, Edgar left. I couldn't breathe because I had three fractured ribs. My boy lifted me up to try and stand up, but I couldn't. I was in so much pain and I couldn't breathe properly. I felt like my back was broken. Eventually

Errol was able to help me walk to the housing at Dufferin Park where his friend lived, and we asked his friend's dad to take me to the hospital.

I didn't want to go to a hospital near home. I was scared that they would call the cops and charge him. I believed he would kill me if he went to jail again. I was so scared. So they drove me and my son to the hospital in Pine Falls. Every time the car bumped it felt like my back was broken. When we got there, all they did was wrap me up and gave me painkillers. They couldn't do anything except give me something for the pain. I don't remember what happened at home after that. It's like a dream. I remember some things but not others.

That same winter I was coming home from work with a little bit of groceries. Before I went inside Donna opened the window from upstairs and said, "Dad is here." She was smiling. "You should see him, how he looks."

He had a big black eye. Somebody fought him, beat him up in a bar. I heard about it after. It was over one of his girlfriends. My kids were saying, "Good enough for him." They saw it as karma. What goes around comes around. They were glad that he got a little bit of his own medicine, my daughter told me later.

I was scared he might take it out on me, but he didn't really do anything to me that time. He just got me to make a phone call. Edgar wanted me to make a date with his girlfriend's ex-husband to make her jealous. I did what I was told and arranged for us to meet at this bar at the West Hotel on Main Street. I was breaking free but slowly. There were times I still had to do as he said to keep me and my kids safe. I was still living in constant fear.

I remember all those times when he would come and threaten me. After he left, I would be paralyzed there, frozen with fear. Then suddenly the phone would ring, and it would be one of my sponsors. "We're picking you up to go to a meeting." Bernelda and Marie. Always those two. Just at the right time. "Diane, you've got to go," they would say.

Sometimes it would be my daughter pushing me. She would say, "Come on, Mum. You're going to that meeting." My daughter Donna supported me so much. She even came with me to a few meetings. She was only about fifteen or sixteen, but Donna was one of my biggest supporters.

The first two or three weeks of leaving an abusive partner is a critical time. It is very crucial that you stay away from them. They can be especially dangerous. The abuser can become even more dangerous than before. They will do anything to try and regain the control they have lost over their partner. I share my personal experience of this with the women I work with today, because I believe it is important to be aware of the danger, while still holding onto the knowledge that you can escape and go on to live a good life. This was my experience after I cut off all contact with Edgar and completely stopped going out on the streets for him. The violence escalated and I nearly lost my children forever.

My youngest son had a terrible accident. Edgar always had guns around; even after I left him, he would stash guns in my house. In so many ways, he made our home unsafe. It killed me that I couldn't keep my kids safe. That day, Randy and his friend were playing with .22 bullets. The boys were hitting bullets with a hammer, and one went right through Randy's eye. Right through. He talks about that today. He talks about how angry he was then, and still is sometimes. He lost his eye because I wasn't home there to take care of him. I was on the run, hiding from Edgar. That's what happened. It hurts, but I listen to him. I understand his pain. He lost his eye.

My daughter took him to the Health Sciences Centre. She was only seventeen, so she wasn't old enough to sign for him to have the surgery needed. They couldn't find me right away because I was hiding at my cousin's place. When I found out he was in the hospital I went there right away.

When I got there I told the nurses, "I've got a restraining order against their dad. If he comes here, or if you see me being taken out of here, call 911. The police are looking for him too." It was useless. He did come. Edgar came there and he found me. He took me right out of there. The nurses didn't do anything. He took me to his car, and he brought me way down Main Street somewhere. He raped me. Then he made me write a letter that said I dropped all charges against him. I jumped out of the car when he was at a stoplight, and I ran to the police station. It was close by. They looked for him, but they couldn't find him.

I wrote that letter because I had to do what he said, or he'd kill me. Later though, when I was free again, I told the police it wasn't true. I was at a point where I knew what I had to do to survive moment to moment, but I was determined that I would not go backwards.

When Randy got out of the hospital, the doctor told me he had to be quiet, to lay still and get lots of rest. I had to really watch him after his eye surgery. We stayed with my friend from Al-Anon in Jig Town, which is down by Burrows. I knew he would be safe there. My teenage kids were still staying at home though, so I would go there each day to take care of them. I would do housework, buy groceries for my kids and all that.

One day, not too long after his surgery, I had to take Randy with me to the house to check on my other kids. Errol and Donna were there with some of their friends, sitting outside. They were teenagers, about sixteen or seventeen, just hanging out. Suddenly, Errol saw his dad and came running in.

"Dad's here!" I didn't have time to run out. I didn't have time to jump; he was already inside. He had a knife. I remember seeing that knife just shining, ready in his hand. He was going to stab me. Errol yelled, "Run Mum, run!" and my son and his friends jumped on him. They saved my life. I ran out with Randy. We jumped into my car and took off. There were so many warrants out for his arrest, and the police were looking for him. I had a restraining order. None of that stopped him from coming after me though.

Not long after that, I went to Safeway after work, and I was going to go drop off some stuff at the house for my kids before going back to my friend's. As I turned my car towards home, I had a strong feeling. Something told me not to go there. In a split second I turned my car down Burrows and went straight to my friend's place. I phoned the house from there. My daughter Sharon answered, and right away I knew something was wrong. He was there. He was sitting there waiting for me with a high-powered rifle. Sharon, Errol, and two of their friends were there in that house, as well as Edgar's girlfriend.

He told the kids that he was going to blow me in half when I walked through that door. They were just praying that I wouldn't come home. I knew. I just had this feeling. I listen to my inner voice. I really believe I was meant to live and that's why I had that feeling.

He grabbed the phone from my daughter, and he said, "If you want to see your kids alive, you better get over here." I didn't say anything. I wrote a note to my friend: *He's at my house.* She ran to the neighbour's and used their phone to call 911. She told them that he was there. They were looking for him. By then he had so many charges against him. I had him on the phone for five, maybe ten minutes before he hung up. Then I heard the cops at my friend's door, and I thought, "Oh God, he must have killed my kids."

"Where's my kids? How's my kids doing?"

The cop just said, "You're coming with us."

I kept screaming and crying in the car to the cops, "Where's my kids? How's my kids doing?"

I kept thinking, "Oh, Christ, they're dead. My kids are dead already." I kept screaming at the cops over and over, "What's going on?"

It was early in the evening when we arrived on Flora. There were at least ten police cars all with their lights going, surrounding the house. He was at the picture window with a rifle pointing out. That's when the cops finally said to me, "We can tell you what's happening now."

They led me to a house nearby where I could be kept safe but still be close to my kids. They were negotiating with him all night. He held my kids as hostages for eleven and a half hours altogether. It was not until the next morning, around eight o'clock, when he finally threw that gun down from the window and gave himself up. Edgar made national news for that hostage holding and was sentenced to three years in prison. That was one of the scariest days of my life.

My youngest daughter, Karen wasn't there when it happened. She was with her cousins on their way to a graduation in Brandon when they heard what was happening on the news. They turned right around and drove as close to the house as they could. She said, "When we got there, the street was full of cops, and it was all blocked on either end of the street. We couldn't find you." Even though she wasn't in the house, the fear that she felt stayed with her forever.

It affected everyone, but I think it hurt Errol the most. After the hostage holding, he started going downhill. He was seventeen years old. Edgar was going to kill them all, and that trauma impacted Errol in a way none of the other experiences before that had. He was never the same after that. Until that point in his life, my son was doing okay. He was working hard in school and had a pretty healthy life. But after his dad did that, he started drinking a lot and doing drugs. To this day he still struggles with it. They were all so traumatized.

9

Seeing the Trees

ONE OF THE MOST important changes I made came shortly
after he went to jail for the hostage holding. I filed for my
divorce. During the hearing the lawyer asked me, "At the
time of the hostage holding," and he named the date, "did
he threaten to kill you? Was he threatening to kill you?"

"Yes."

I remember the judge just looking at me. "Is that true?"

"Yes."

He slapped his hand on the desk. "Divorce granted."
"Divorce granted," he proclaimed, making the official stamp.
No problem. I got my divorce right away. He understood.
He didn't need to hear anymore. They knew Edgar's history
and that was enough.

For years my kids were angry with me for not leaving
him, and after the divorce they were angry with me for the
divorce too. It was very confusing for them. I never blamed
them for it. I know that leaving him was the right thing.
Despite their confusion at the time, I know they felt that as
well. Years later my youngest daughter said to me, "I was so
proud of you for being able to leave him, Mum." They knew
how dangerous and controlling he was, and I think they
understood how hard it was to make that break.

There was still fear, but it no longer held me back. I lived from moment to moment, and when the fear would creep in and I found myself wondering what would happen when he was released, I told myself, "I'll deal with it when the time comes." I became stronger and stronger. Bernelda really encouraged me to do service work in the self-help group, which really helped me spiritually. She introduced me to the open speaker meeting, and I got my year cake. Bernelda said I grew fast in the program. She said I reminded her of a small rosebud that fully bloomed in just a short while. It was in big part because of her support that I was finally able to make that break. I thought I would never do it, but I did. It didn't take very long after finding that kind of support that I was able to find the courage to change even more things in my life. I really value Al-Anon and where it took me. It taught me how to live one day at a time, although in the beginning I had to shrink that to minutes and even seconds just to be able to live and not worry about Edgar – to be able to carry on without fearing what he'd do to me when he got out of jail.

A lot of my memories come to me when I'm on the road, driving and listening to music. I can't stop all the time and start writing, so by the time I get where I'm going, I often forget. The memory is just gone. I don't worry about it though. If it's meant to be, it'll come back again. Driving on Highway 59 or Highway 11 can trigger painful memories for me. After I left Edgar, and when he was in jail, I was living in Winnipeg. I used to go down to my reserve pretty often, but it took me about two years before I could travel there without breaking down. I was still filled with fear. I used to dread going to Sagkeeng because of what he would do to me along that road.

Then one day, there was a moment that changed how I saw things forever. I don't know exactly where I was, but I was driving down Highway 59, and suddenly I noticed the water

and trees around me. I thought, "Man, this is beautiful."
I guess for me that was a spiritual awakening. I began to
appreciate my surroundings. I had never really even seen
these things before. It was like I had been living with tunnel
vision for all those years. When I was finally free and well
enough to do more than just survive, I truly began to heal.

I started living with someone shortly after my divorce.
I had met Jon when I was still working the streets for Edgar.
Jon wasn't ever my trick. He used to take care of me. He
would bring me coffee and let me warm up in his car in the
wintertime. He used to talk to me. He used to tease me,
"Come here, my darling." I thought he was homely, and I'd
say, "Oh, get out of here you ugly thing." That's how I talked
to him, and yet he really cared for me.

Jon had this friend who was a pilot. One night, back when
I was still working on the streets for Edgar, they were sitting
there, watching me getting in and out of cars. He said to his
friend, "She's going to be my wife someday. She's going to
straighten out and we'll get married."

Jon really loved me, even though he knew what I did
before. He loved me and he loved my kids. He was really nice
to my kids. After we started living with him, he would help
me discipline them and teach them things. He was putting
food on the table and helping me financially with the kids.
I had three of them at home then. He truly loved and cared
for all my kids. I was in love and felt loved for the first time.

Edgar didn't just let me go though, even with the divorce
and his being locked up. Even from jail he tried to control
me. He got his girlfriend to call the welfare office and report
me for fraud. They called me down to the office for a meeting.
I saw my file. There were all these newspaper clippings and
receipts there. Edgar had given them the proof that I bought
a brand new car without reporting it and that I was working
all those years while collecting welfare.

I had been doing housework for the past ten years. Edgar
used to drop me off and pick me up from this one job where
I worked for a lady on Queen Street. I worked for that lady
for at least five years. I had steady work and would earn
around thirty dollars a day. If I did two places, sometimes
I'd make sixty bucks. He took all the money. He had a bank
account at TD where he put the money that he got from me.
He never worked. He always had us on welfare. I used to
have to lie to them about everything. I had to tell them that
he wasn't living with us and pretend I wasn't working because
they would have forced him to work or cut us off. He collected
from me, and he collected from them.

I was listening to that welfare worker go through all this
proof against me, and when she finished, she said, "What do
you have to say?"

I was resigned to the fact that I was going to be punished
for what Edgar made me do, but I was also at a place in my
life where I was finally ready to stand up for myself. "Well,"
I said, "first of all, I'm not planning to stay on welfare. I'm
already looking for a new job. I'm going to start working, so
if you cut me off, fine." I didn't want to be on welfare anyway.
I had already applied for a job at the Health Sciences Centre,
a hospital in Winnipeg. I was pretty sure I was going to get it.

"You can do whatever you want with me, but I'm going to
tell you something," I said. "What Edgar didn't share with
you was that he was the one taking all the money. I was
paying for his brand new car. He registered that car in my
name and put that he was living in Selkirk at his mother's
address. He was the one driving the car. He lied about his
address. He lied about everything. He was living with us,
plus he was living with another woman at the same time, and
getting money off me. What he didn't tell you is that he put
me on the street, and he made me steal. He made me lie.

He took all the money. I had nothing. My kids had nothing. Now because I'm not doing that for him anymore, he's mad and he's telling you that I committed fraud. But he didn't tell you everything. You can put me in jail, charge me if you have to. But I'll come out clean and I'll start a new life."

They didn't charge me. They let everything go. They said, "Thank you for being honest." They offered me another month to help me out and told me to let them know when I was working. That's what happened, and I was on my own from that point forward. I didn't have to steal anymore. I didn't have to go out on the street. I could work and know that the money I earned would be mine. I worked hard. I shopped in thrift stores for myself and my kids and made sure we had everything we needed. I really had a good life then. It was so different. My life took on a whole different meaning.

I really learned fast, being in Al-Anon. They never told me what to do, but they guided me nonetheless. They helped me find my own way at my own pace. I became empowered. I took to heart the teachings they gave me, the Serenity Prayer and all the readings. I was doing a lot of reading in the Al-Anon book and other self-help books. Louise Hayes was one of my favourite authors. I read *You Can Heal Your Life* and *Heal Your Body*. Healing books like that had a powerful influence on me. It was like self-counselling. I spent a lot of time with my sponsors, especially Bernelda, Marie, and Vera, who gave me a lot of encouragement and showed me how our Anishinabe culture could provide the healing and strength I was finally ready for.

I attended the Four Worlds workshop, where I got to work with many incredible Elders. So much happened during the seven days I was there. I experienced lots of healing. I began to embrace my culture and traditional ways. I did a lot of travelling in those days, attending teaching lodges, picking

sacred medicines, and going to powwows and other
ceremonies. This part of my healing journey was very
powerful. It was what I needed. I had the opportunity to
attend ceremonies in Saskatchewan, and I got to dance
at round dances and learn the sacred teachings. I was so
fortunate to have good friends to walk with me on my new
path. I knew this was the most powerful way of healing.

The Sweat Lodge really helped me. I used to have
claustrophobia because of what happened to me at residential
school. One of the punishments I was put through was
getting locked up in dark places. One place was in the
washroom in the basement, and another was under the stairs.
I was put there about three times. It was completely dark in
there, and I was terrified. I remember thinking I was going
to die in there. I thought my body would be rotten before
my papa would find me there. I was really traumatized.
Years later, I was still affected by it.

Before going into the Sweat Lodge for the first time,
I shared my fears with Vera, who brought me there. She
sat beside me in the Sweat Lodge and helped me to work
through them. It's pitch black in there, and it's hot. Each
time I had these two Elders, my friends, in there with me.
They would gently tap my knee and say to me, "You will be
fine." And they would calm me down. And I went through
it. Sometimes they would have to open the door and let me
out. I was badly damaged by what happened in school. But
I knew I had to keep going to these ceremonies, to these
Sweats. I knew they were good. In time I was able to go on
my own. I did a lot of crying and releasing in there because
I carried so much pain. Now, instead of being afraid of dark,
enclosed spaces, I feel comfortable because I associate it
with the healing of the Sweat Lodge instead of the pain of
my past. That's one of the reasons why I really believe in
that way of healing, the traditional way of healing.

My first experience with the Sundance Ceremony was on the Pine Ridge Reserve in 1979. I travelled there with Vera and Bernelda. I had Randy with me. I always took my younger son with me. I know that is why today he has a strong desire to follow his traditional ways of life and of healing. This was where I first received sacred teachings about the Sundance Ceremony and fasting. I observed a lot of healing happening. People were crying, dancing around that circle. I was crying when I saw them and saw the tree of life. I participated in the fasting for three and a half days and joined in the feast on the last day of the ceremonies. It was such an incredible experience. I drove all night and went to work the next day. I wasn't even tired. I had lots of energy. That was a very powerful experience.

I had another opportunity to attend Sundance Ceremonies in Rocky Mountain, Alberta. I travelled with Juliana and her husband, my brother-in-law, who was a respected Elder. There were tents all in a big circle, and the Sundance Lodge made of poplar trees was in the middle. We stayed in one of six tipis for guests. I really admired the Elder that led the ceremonies there. The drumming and songs would go on all day, from sunrise to sunset. Listening to the drums was very healing to my hard soul. We would gather in the evening and early morning around the fire and listen to teachings shared and some funny stories. There was a lot of laughter. I had a lot of fun learning and healing. I was very fortunate to be around Elders in the community. My spirit became stronger and stronger every time I participated in ceremonies like this one.

I had the hunger now, the desire to start dancing, but I didn't start until some years later. I think I was afraid of it – worried I wouldn't be able to make it. I had rheumatoid arthritis, and I had a hard time walking. I didn't know if I could go for that long. Dancing for four days without food and water seemed impossible, but after seeking counsel and guidance from the Elders I felt confident. I did a lot of crying when I danced. I was blinded with tears looking at that tree. You have to look at that tree in the centre of the circle all day long while you're dancing. You have little breaks, like ten-minute breaks, and then they start singing again. The healing songs with the drum start and you have to stand and look at that tree. You can't look anywhere else. Painful thoughts would come into my mind. I felt excruciating emotional pain. That's when I would pray really hard. That's what I was advised to do by that Elder. Keep on praying, keep on dancing, keep that energy moving.

I cried for three days. It was the most powerful experience in my healing journey. I can't even describe that feeling. At the end of the four-day ceremony you go and you hold the tree. There are a bunch of people that were dancing around that circle. I didn't know that my relatives were there to support me. My sister, my brother-in-law, and my nephew and niece had their hands on me as I was holding that tree. There again, I did a lot of crying. I felt weak from all that crying, but after the ceremony I knew there was hope. I was able to complete the four days with ease. I could have danced another four days, that's how much energy I had. It was a powerful healing ceremony. I looked forward to the next one and the next.

I was growing spiritually, but I realized I needed more healing. I continued to carry a lot of hurt and pain and anger, and I knew that all those feelings were hurting me. I started going to Haid Smith Counselling. I was fortunate that it was covered back then. They're very expensive. I wish my kids could see them. They're very good. But there just isn't enough coverage. They worked with me for over two years. I did a lot of intense inner-child work there. I dealt with my anger there. I did a lot of releasing there by hitting a block and using other strategies they taught me. I carried a lot of anger, right from when I was a child. Hurt turns to anger, and I carried a lot of anger.

Sometimes I don't know what was worse, my life with Edgar or all the abuse and pain of my childhood. I want to say it was all the same, but then it seems like I'm able to talk about what I went through with Edgar, and I struggle when I want to talk about what happened to me as a child. I did a lot of work to deal with the core of the trauma, but there are still some walls up in my mind, trying to protect that little girl who had no protection then. When I allow myself to remember those things, it feels like they are happening all over again. I still have healing to do in this area of my life.

So many people wanted to help me, and I finally let them. Maybe my Spirit Guides told me I needed to accept the help all these good people in my life were offering me. One of the people who really helped me was my sister Juliana.

One day we were having a visit and she said to me, "I know you made a lot of changes with going to Al-Anon, but I want you to see this chiropractor." In the past I would have brushed her off, but this time I decided to trust in my sister and accept the help she was offering me.

I went to Dr. Marcoux's office where he and Dr. D. Feasey did chiropractic work on me. In the beginning I went two or three times a week. I did a lot of releasing there. I had suffered from inflammation pain, and the treatments helped a lot. For the first two years I did a lot of crying and laughing on the table. It was much needed, as I carried a lot of pain and rage that affected me physically. I continue to go there to this day.

I made a lot of positive changes in my life. I got the job at the Health Sciences Centre in the housekeeping department. I continued to attend healing ceremonies during my holidays. There was a lot of racism at that hospital, but I was already becoming spiritually strong, and I was able to handle anything that came my way there. A lot of my co-workers took a liking to me, even in the management department. I carried a new, positive energy that I think people appreciated.

I started going to classes, and before long I graduated with my GED for Grade 12. I had always wanted to have a career but could never do anything to better myself because of Edgar. I was determined to do it now. I wasn't sure what I was meant to do, but I knew even then that I wanted to help people. I figured I'd go into nursing, but I became interested in working in addiction counselling after doing some volunteer work with what is now the Addictions Foundation of Manitoba.

Through Al-Anon I had been learning about alcoholism, and I was beginning to understand how it had affected my family. I made my decision and went after my goals, with the support of my sponsor Bernelda. After two years' training, I completed my formal education to become a counsellor. I continued to go to different healing workshops through the years. Throughout those years and all the years that followed I have continued to work on my healing and embrace every opportunity to learn and grow.

Edgar never left me alone, but I was stronger by the time he was released. He was out on probation after only a year and a half, free to harass me again. He had found out I was living with somebody else before he was even released from prison because he had people watching me. He was furious about it. He phoned me one day, shortly after his release, and started saying things about Jon and making threats. He was calling Jon white trash and accusing him of being mean to his kids. He said, "No one is going to get away with this." He went on and on, calling me down. "He's just using you, you ugly—"

"Are you finished?" I cut him off. For the first time in my life, I stood up to him. I said, "That 'white trash' I'm living with is putting food on the table and clothes on your kids' back – something you never did in the eighteen years that I was with you. You lived off of us, you fucking bum."

I went on, "One more phone call out of you and you'll be back in the slammer. I'm gonna call your probation officer. Just leave me alone. Now put that in your pipe and smoke it if you have one." Then I just hung up. That was how I talked to him. I was done with taking his abuse.

The next morning my back windshield was smashed, and my four tires were slashed. The same thing with my partner's car; all his tires were slashed too. There was no doubt about who did it. Edgar would do things like that. That was his style when he was mad at someone. "The way you hurt the white man is with money," he used to say. I knew it was him by the way he thought.

Jon and I were sitting at the table, getting ready to go to work that morning. Jon was upset, of course. I said, "You know what? No use getting upset. It happened. Let's just deal with it. We know the person who did this is really unhappy, and we're happy with our lives. We'll just buy new tires." I was ready to move on. I was ready to embrace happiness.

Jon is the only man I can say I ever truly loved in my life. He is a good man. He loved my kids, and he was good to us. In the end he broke my heart. He was so insecure with me. He would say, years later, when we became friends again, "I was always afraid you'd meet somebody else and leave me."

I had lots of friends. There were a lot of good people in my life, and he was afraid. He didn't trust me because of my life before. As we got on in age, his insecurities got worse. I used to tell him, "You know what Jon? I really love you.

I'll always be faithful to you." But that wasn't good enough. He cheated on me. I suppose he did it because it was what he expected me to do. I loved him and I understood why he did what he did, but I left him. Even though I was still learning, and I still had a long way to go before I was healthy, I knew I deserved better.

I guess it was meant to be that way. To this day we're friends and he always asks how my kids are doing when we talk. He really loves them. I know he loves me, too, but I'd never take him back. I know now that I am worth more than that. I deserve someone who is secure enough to trust me and remain faithful to me. It took me a long time to see it, but I know now that I am worthwhile.

After things ended with Jon, I had another unhealthy relationship. It didn't really mean anything, and I knew it would never go anywhere. It was just a convenience kind of thing. Even as an adult I was still like a needy child and still so damaged. I realized I still wasn't a healthy person. I still had a lot of work to do on myself. I attracted those kinds of people who were insecure and weren't healthy either. I learned from these experiences though, and I never again put up with any sort of abuse in my life. Never again.

Today, I have high standards. I guess that's why I'm alone now. At my age there are still some people who are interested in me, but I'm not interested in them. I have a sense of self-worth that I never used to have. I get to be picky because I deserve to be with someone I truly love and who truly loves me. I'm also okay alone. I know that I can take care of myself and be happy. It took me a long time to get to this point, but I was already beginning to understand my worth when I left Jon.

One of the most important tools I was given that helped me with this was the power of positive affirmations. This teaching came from a nurse named Lily and her husband

Richard, who were doing Reiki on me. I was laying on that table, and they were moving energy and pain from my body.

Lily told me, "Diane, I want you to say: 'I am a wonderful, worthwhile, beautiful person.'"

I couldn't say it. I had very low self-esteem from being called down all the time. It began when I was just a kid and continued throughout my young adulthood. From my mama and from the nuns at school, the message was always the same: "You're worthless and you'll never amount to anything." Then Edgar would keep me down; never calling me by my name, but always "Hey, stupid," or "Hey, bean-brain." She had to tell me about three times before I said it. I broke down and I started crying. All my life I had been told and truly believed that I was worthless, not good enough. It was painful to say those words: "I am a wonderful, worthwhile, beautiful person." But it worked. Eventually it worked. They told me I had to say those positive affirmations all the time, and to this day I continue to practise and share that teaching with the people I work with. I became so interested in Reiki that I took the training to practise it. It wasn't covered and I had to pay for it myself, but it was worth it. I really believe in it.

I learned a lot about myself and life during those first few years of freedom. I embraced the healing journey with all my heart and never gave up on myself. I learned how to love and to be loved. I learned how to be a better mother to my children. I learned that I was a worthwhile and beautiful person. I found my calling as a counsellor and embraced my culture. Leaving Edgar and standing up to him was terrifying and truly dangerous. I nearly lost my life and the lives of my children, but we survived. We survived, and we were finally free. He was still around and could still hurt us, but I had a new strength and good people in my life to help us through whatever came our way.

10

Freedom at Last

IN 1986 EDGAR WAS sentenced to life in prison for the murder of an RCMP officer. Two days before it happened, I was at a training. I was sitting with some co-workers when I got a strange feeling suddenly. It was just like when he held my kids hostage. "You know, guys," I said, "something is going to happen, something tragic. I just hope it's none of us."

Two days later I heard Edgar shot two cops. Edgar had always hated cops. He used to say, "I'm going to take a few of them with me when I go." It was a young Anishinabe man that he killed. He wounded the other one. I guess that man was in a wheelchair for the rest of his life. He was from Newfoundland. I think he moved back over there after the shooting. I heard that he died some years ago, but I don't know if that's true. After shooting those cops, Edgar went to Harry Fontaine's place, who was living with Edgar's ex. He held them hostage and was going to kill them, but a neighbour called the police, and he was finally arrested.

Edgar was sent to Stony Mountain for life. My kids put my own feelings into words when they expressed theirs. When we heard the news they said, "He's never going to get out of jail now. He's never going to hurt anyone again." We were all thinking the same thing. I felt really bad for the officers and the family of that young cop he killed, but at the same time we were overcome with relief. We were finally safe. The world was a safer place for everyone with Edgar behind bars. He was a murderer. One of Edgar's nieces told me something disturbing about Edgar, years after he was gone, that linked him to yet another murder. She had married a white guy and lived somewhere in Transcona. One of her husband's friends was a detective. One day, sometime in the early 1970s, that detective asked her, "Do you know Edgar Olson?"

She said, "Yeah. I'm ashamed to say that's my uncle."

The detective said, "You know those two kids that just got killed? You know, the ones that were shot in the back as they were running for their lives in a field by Garven Road. We know it was Edgar who did it, but we can't prove it. There's no hard evidence, but we know it's him."

They linked Edgar to the killing because apparently one of the kids that was killed was a judge's son or daughter. The judge had charged Edgar for something or other, and Edgar always used to say, "Anyone who puts me in jail will pay for it with their life and the lives of anyone they care about." I have no way of knowing for sure whether Edgar was the one who killed them. There may not be any evidence, and I only heard about this as second-hand information, but I believe it. Edgar was a murderer, and I have no reason to doubt the story. It wasn't the only one, after all.

Another incident I heard about happened in the early 1980s. Edgar was stabbed coming out of the bar on Sutherland Avenue. I remember him being in the hospital after it happened. I was told that the man who stabbed him was the brother of the guy Edgar murdered in '69. From that point on Edgar started to follow that guy around. He was out for that guy. Edgar told me how he followed the bus he was riding in: "Now I know where he lives." Edgar said

that. He was going to do away with him. "Now I know where
he lives. He doesn't even know I followed him. I know which
house. He'll disappear and they'll never know." Not long
after that, I heard that man had moved to Calgary. A few
years later he was killed on the street. To this day, they don't
know who did it. It is an unsolved murder. I am sure it was
Edgar who killed him too.

Edgar used to be gone for days. He'd go with his friend
Derek. Derek knew a lot of his secrets. Edgar trusted him.
Sometimes I would hear them talking. So I knew a lot of his
secrets too. I may not have known who Edgar was when I
married him, but years of living with him and being abused
by him taught me what a psychopath he really was.

I experienced a freedom like never before after Edgar was
sent to Stony Mountain. There was security in knowing he
was there for life and wouldn't be able to come out and torture
me or my kids anymore. Still, he persisted in communicating
with me. He sent tapes and letters all the time. I had always
thought Edgar was a good singer. He played guitar and
sang Hank Williams songs. I remember one evening, early in
our relationship when we were sitting down the bank by the
river. It was getting dark, and he had his guitar. He sang
the song "The Waltz of the Wind" by Hank Williams. At the
time I was impressed. He never really sang in public, but
he would sing to me a lot. After he was sent to jail for life, he
sent me tapes. On one of them he sang, "Take these Chains
from My Heart." That was one of the songs. He sang a few
songs on that tape, dedicating them to me. He talked to me
on that tape too. I didn't keep it though. I was still very
angry and wanted nothing to do with him.

By the time Edgar went to prison he had about seven
kids with other women on top of our five children. Before he
was sent away, he was living with a woman and their son.
Apparently, Edgar treated her the same way he treated me.

She went through a lot of the same stuff that I did. He put her on the street. I saw her there, and I know how he was. He was also sleeping with his stepdaughter. My son saw it and told me. His son from that relationship committed suicide some years ago. He was the same age as Randy. They were so close in age; they could have been twins. He had a relationship with my kids. They would get together sometimes and talk about their dad.

That was how we found out that his mom, Edgar's girlfriend, was smuggling pills into the prison for him during her visits. Edgar couldn't handle prison. Six years into his life sentence, he was being investigated for something. I think that's one of the reasons he killed himself. Mainly, I think he couldn't handle it, being in there. He saved up the pills his girlfriend was bringing in and he took them all at once. Edgar was gone.

After he died, I drove with my daughter to Stony Mountain to pick up his stuff. There was a worker at the jail who told us what happened. She told us it was a suicide and offered to show us his letter. Neither my daughter nor I wanted to read it. It's best that she didn't see it. I think it would have been too much for her. We didn't need anything from him.

When he died, my kids had lots of mixed feelings. They can talk about it with me now. I remember how it affected my kids when they saw the headline in the *Free Press*: "Cop Killer Commits Suicide in Stony Mountain." That hurt my kids even though they had a bad life with him. They were happy that he was gone, but he was their dad, and they still loved him. They felt guilty for being glad he was gone. I understand how they felt because I struggled with my own conflicting emotions at that time too.

I asked my sister, "Why am I crying? I'm not even sorry he's gone." I no longer resented him for everything he put me through, but he did us a favour by dying and I knew it.

"Painful memories," she said. "You're crying over all the things you went through, that's all." She understood what I couldn't at the time. I was crying because for so long I had lived in pain and fear. Now that he was gone, I was free to grieve – not for the loss of his life, but the life that he had taken from me; the life I could now reclaim.

That said, even in death his actions continued to harm his family. Even beyond the psychological trauma that we were working through, we were also still being denied our rights and forced to move forward without any kind of support from our community. There was bad blood between him and some of the people in charge in Scanterbury at the time, so when I went to ask for help to pay for his funeral, I was refused. I brought my daughter there with me. I wanted them to understand that the funeral wasn't so much for Edgar as for his kids; but the woman I spoke to just sat there with her arms crossed. She shook her head and said, "No."

I wasn't surprised that they were refusing to help us, and I didn't push it. I said to my daughter, "That's fine, that's okay. We don't need them." But we couldn't afford a funeral and I wanted closure for my kids. I decided to go to Sagkeeng for help. Jerry Fontaine was chief then and didn't hesitate in helping us. He understood that this was for me and my kids, not for Edgar.

We had the funeral there. My kids and I were there, and my friend Mimi and a few others came. Even the father of the cop Edgar killed was there. I went up to him and shook his hand. He did a write up in the paper not long after that. He wrote about meeting the family of the man who killed his son. He said, "It's sad, the ones left behind." For all his grief, he was able to empathize with what my family and I were going through. I was very touched and I have a lot of respect for him.

My kids suffered so much. They ended up paying for the damage and pain Edgar caused, even years after he was gone.

No one in Scanterbury wanted to help my kids because Edgar had hurt so many people there. It was up to me to support them, even as I was just starting to get back on my feet. It was nothing new. We were always denied help from Scanterbury, even though we had rights as band members there. We were always denied help, whether it was for dental work or schooling. Eventually I just gave up trying. What was the point? I understood that if Mrs. Pine or her family had any control there we wouldn't get a thing. Edgar killed her brother, and my kids and I would keep paying for that. If I had known it was an option I would have transferred my band membership back to Sagkeeng. My kids could have done that too. I would have got the help I needed if I had.

When Donna graduated from college with a degree in business administration, we were invited to the graduation celebration in Scanterbury. She had done really well, and I was so proud of her. She had the highest grades of all the students. She felt that a lot of students were taking advantage of their free education and abusing the system. It made her work extra hard, wanting to be different, and she excelled. We were invited by Southeast Child and Family Services to this dinner celebrating the college graduates that year. We went thinking that she would be honoured in some way for her high achievement and success in school. Everybody was all dressed up and we felt kind of poor by comparison, but we were still proud.

The band began handing out roses and gifts to all the graduates. Even the graduates with low grades got cheques, but my daughter, who had done better than anyone there, got nothing. She turned to me with tears rolling down her cheeks and said to me, "Not even a fucking rose, Mum."

"It's okay, Donna," I said, even though it broke my heart and I almost cried too. I wanted to be strong for her. She was doing so well, and I didn't want her to feel hurt or hard done by. I didn't want to see her held back or pushed down because of who her father was. I wanted her to overcome and thrive in the life she chose for herself.

She was already looking for a job, and she needed nice clothes to wear to interviews, so we went back to Sagkeeng to see Jerry at the band office. I told him a little bit about what had happened. I didn't ask for anything, but right away he turned to Donna and asked her, "How much money will you need? Will five hundred do?" My girl was so happy. He had made her feel special and deserving, and he had given her all that she needed to start off on the right foot.

As soon as we left the band office she exclaimed through happy tears, "Oh, Mum!" She just hugged me and gave me a kiss on the cheek.

I hugged her back and said, "You shoulda done that to Jerry. You shoulda gave him a hug!"

"Yeah, I know," she said.

I joked, "You should have told him you needed a thousand. He probably would have given it to you."

I've always liked Jerry. He was always so kind to me and my family, and he never let our connection to Edgar stop him from taking care of us when we needed it.

Donna and I went out and spent all that money shopping for professional clothing and shoes that she would need to go on interviews and to wear once she started working. She got a job working for Southeast Child and Family Services and was excited to be starting her career. She didn't have good luck though. She was abused there and suffered under the politics that went on. There was a lot of stress, and she was having a really hard time there. Then she got into a really bad car accident. It made the front page of the paper.

She tried to beat a train. She wasn't drunk, but she did have a drink before driving, and she made a terrible decision that nearly cost her life. She tried to beat a train and get across some tracks. The train hit her. It dragged her about one block. Looking at the car, you would think that no one inside it could have lived. My girl survived but she had a bad head injury. She was never the same after that. She was not the same person after that accident. My hardworking girl would never be the same again. She got hooked on her pain meds and continues to struggle with her addiction to this day.

My kids talk about what we went through sometimes. One time Randy said, "I was over at my friend's and his parents were partying. We were upstairs, and I was a bit uncomfortable because I was just waiting for a big fight to break out. I expected his dad to go nuts and start smashing things," he said. "I thought that was the normal way. I thought that everybody was like that. But he didn't. His parents weren't like that. His dad wasn't like that. He was nice." To Randy that wasn't normal. It really hurt that my son felt that way. It was so much like my own perceptions of my childhood, how I normalized abuse.

My kids have clearer memories of those years than I do. Sometimes they will bring up things and I have absolutely no recollection. They're always trying to jog my memory: "Don't you remember anything?" I can't. There are a lot of things I don't remember that my kids mention. Even the good stuff, the happy times. Things like school concerts, or hockey games, or something nice that happened. I don't remember those things. I have no memory of it at all.

Around twenty-five years ago, when I went to the Four Worlds workshop, I asked one Elder when they were praying over me, "Why is it I can't remember anything?"

He said, "Because the Creator only puts enough on your plate for right now. There's too much." I understand that today. I went through too much to process everything at once. So I only remember what I can think about and work through. It's like post-traumatic stress. I've done lots and

lots of work over the years, but still so much of my life is a
blank. When I'm ready, more will come.

My kids know all about my life. I thought they didn't know
that I worked on the streets, but they all did. I guess after a
while, they each found out. One morning when I was visiting
with my youngest daughter, she told me how she knew. I
think she was the first to talk about it. Later, I asked my oldest
daughter how she found out. She said, "Because Dad put a
private line in the bedroom for your customers to call you on.
He used to unplug it, but one time I plugged it in when you
were both out and answered it. It was one of your customers.
That was when I knew for sure what was happening."

Randy knows too. We never talked about it, but a few
summers ago he was laughing about some hookers on the
street. It hurt me. I said, "You know, you shouldn't make fun
of them. You don't know their lives. You don't know who put
them there, or why they're there. Did you know that your dad
put me on the street?"

He went quiet. He said, "Yeah."

"Well, don't do that," I said. "Don't laugh at those girls.
You don't know their story." So he never does that anymore.

I wish I had more money so I could help my kids more.
They're always struggling financially. Sharon had the worst
of it. She was even homeless at one time. Her physical and
mental health were affected by her trauma, and she became
addicted to drugs. She was always very vulnerable. She was
always getting beaten up and taken advantage of by people.
Right up until the day she died my daughter blamed me
for what happened to her. She said I knew. Several years
ago, when I was in a training on child abuse, I asked one
of the workers, "How come my daughter still believes him
and not me?"

She answered, "Because in her eyes you were the adult,
and you were supposed to know. Kids are very vulnerable.

They believe what they're told. Her dad told her that you knew, so she believes that to this day."

Many times, I sent her to treatment centres to help her with her addictions and to deal with her issues. I sent her for treatment in Edmonton and to Nechi Institute twice. I made referrals; I worked hard to get her the services and help she needed throughout the years. I loved and supported her the best I could, but in the end we lost her.

My youngest daughter isn't doing too badly. She's got a good husband, and she always worked. Once she told me that when she was sixteen, she made up her mind that she wasn't going to depend on me. She's very independent despite everything that has happened.

My youngest son's mental health has suffered because of all the trauma in his childhood as well. He was diagnosed with PTSD. Like me, my kids struggled to learn in school and have very low self-esteem because of all the trauma. Randy doesn't have a steady job, but he does a lot of temporary jobs. He works hard. As I write this, he's got a job painting a whole house, so for the next two weeks he's got something. The other day he picked me up from shopping and came to my place for coffee. His wife phoned him, and he was joking with her. He said, "Okay, my queen. Okay, my queen. What else do you want, my queen?" He was just teasing her because it's almost like he's at her beck and call. That was the phrase he used. "I'm at your beck and call all the time, my darling." He was just joking, but it's pretty clear that she's the boss.

After that he said to me, "Sometimes I would like to keep some money for myself."

Laughing, I said, "Well, maybe hide it."

"I tried that once," he said. "When I go to sleep, she digs around in my pockets. Then, when I try to get mad at her for taking my money, she just laughs and says, 'Don't you dare get mad. You're supposed to give me all the money. That's the way it's supposed to be.'"

I laugh at him when he tells me stuff like that because he's so funny. Randy's still got some issues. He gets mad and yells a lot, but he loves his wife and he's never violent with her. It makes me happy because it really shows how different he is from his dad. That is one thing I really like about my boys. Neither of them is violent. I used to worry that they'd turn out like Edgar, but when I see my youngest son and the way he is with his wife, I don't worry anymore.

Randy is always there for me. Now that I'm older and not well, he takes care of me. He's always bringing me groceries and taking me to appointments. I rely on him a lot. He's also good to his kids. He spoils them. He just loves them so much, and so do I. My little grandkids are just so cute. Most of my grandkids are struggling because of the aftermath of all the trauma my kids and I went through, but I hope that my kids will continue to work through their pain the way I have, and my grandkids will be okay.

I've had a lot of hard lessons. Watching my children suffer has been the hardest part of my journey. Still, I know that Edgar was meant to be in my life. All the things that happened to me happened for a reason. That's how I look at it today. Everything I went through, I lived through. I survived. I know I still have a lot of pain inside, even after all the work and the healing that I did. It's still very painful. I guess I'll die like that. It will always be there, but at least I'm not messed up anymore. There was a time I couldn't function. Now I live with my pain. I've thrived in spite of it, or maybe even because of it.

I always wanted to be happy and to do good; I just didn't know how. For so long I pushed people away, believing I could do it alone, that I didn't need anybody. I think the real reason I couldn't accept help for so long was because

I didn't believe I deserved anything better. My first step towards healing was about survival. I accepted help because I didn't want to die, but I had no idea how help could change my life beyond simple preservation.

Al-Anon and the incredible people I met there gave me the courage and strength to break away. More importantly, with their help I became empowered and began to develop my self-worth. I became aware that I needed and deserved more. I had to do more healing. Before long I was embracing every healing and self-improvement opportunity that crossed my path. I was hurt in every way. My mind, my body, my spirit, and my emotional well-being were all incredibly damaged from a lifetime of abuse. I needed to approach my healing in a holistic way, or I would never find balance. I accepted help from all corners, and it completely changed my life. I came out of the darkness and into the light. Understanding came, and with that came forgiveness. It was a whole new world for me.

I can smile now, and I am filled with gratitude, not only for all the help I have received but also for the suffering. I experienced it all for a reason; I have compassion and purpose because of it. I am grateful, but sometimes I still cry and am filled with hurt. Countless times I was brutally beaten and left for dead. For so much of my life I felt utterly alone and unloved. So I still cry despite of all the healing, ceremonies, inner-child work, and therapy. That is why I do what I call "maintenance" on myself to this day. I know right away when I need something because I'm really in tune with my body. I notice when tension or hurt is building inside of me. My breathing changes, for one thing, and there are lots of other subtle things I can feel. My body tells me that I need help, and I listen. I do ceremony or go to see either Dr. Marcoux or Dr. Feasey. I have friends I can talk to whenever I need to. Whatever I do, I get the help I need right away.

As I continue my healing, I try to share what I've been through and what I've learned with the people I work with. I believe that I was meant to live through it all so that I could use my experiences to help others, and I have dedicated myself to doing so throughout my career as a counsellor. I share my experiences and everything I have learned over the years with the clients I work with. I used a lot of healing methods in my journey. All those things that I used really helped me, and I know they can help others too.

A few years ago, I worked with a family that really stood out to me. It was a single mother who had a son and daughter. She favoured her daughter, and the boy really misbehaved. Her situation reminded me of Edgar and the stories I heard from his childhood. The favouritism his mom showed for his sister caused a lot of trauma, which affected them all gravely. I used that scenario when I worked with this family at the treatment centre in Sagkeeng a few years ago. I encouraged the mother to change. I told her, "You treat your son fairly, show him love, you know, not only your daughter." That boy had already developed some serious issues. You could see that he might always want to hurt his sister, but change was happening. As his mother began to change and treat them fairly and give him the love and attention he needed, he, too, began to change. I use my life experience to help people, though I don't always tell them the details. I use the teachings that I gained from the experiences. So there's some good comes out of bad.

I'm still working at my age. I'm over eighty years old and still working. People are always telling me to rest, but I don't think I ever will. I am doing what I am meant to do. Right now, I'm working in a women's shelter. I counsel women who have gone through abuse and all kinds of stuff. I can relate to a lot of the stories they tell me. I can always relate to their stories. Maybe that's why I have a need to give back, why I know I can help. I appreciate life. I'm happy. I'm grateful today for my life. I've had lots of struggles and lots of pain, but I'm happy today. I don't have much, but I'm happy with what I have.

I'm trying to write this story because I want to give women hope. I want them to know what I went through and how terrified and hurt I was, because I want them to know they are not alone. More importantly, I want them to know that there is hope. I was able to make that break and have a good life. I want them to know it can be done so that they will have hope for themselves. To do that I have to face my past bravely and share everything. It is what I have always done in my work as a counsellor and what I am doing now through this book.

Telling my story has been another form of therapy for me, and another way that I can reach out and help others. It has forced me to remember and delve into things in my life I have hidden from. At times it felt like I was reliving my past, and it was so painful that I wanted to stop. Often, I thought I couldn't go through with it. Talking about this stuff is just so painful. I am strong though, and I have not given up. I have laughed and cried, shrunk down, and stood tall as I faced my past. It has taken strength and bravery. I took care of myself and let others take care of me as I sifted through my painful past. That is healing. Healing is hard and hopeful all at once. It is continuous, never-ending, but constantly rewarding too. I am looking forward to the next stage of this journey, the process of letting it go. I find peace in knowing that my story will give hope to others like me.

ACKNOWLEDGMENTS

I WOULD LIKE TO acknowledge my great appreciation for the many people who helped me through some of the greatest challenges in my life and who helped me realize my dream of sharing my story with the world.

A sincere thank you to Alvin Toll, the probation officer who saved my life by introducing me to Al-Anon. I will always remember what he said to me that day. He said, "Diane, I want you to start going to these meetings. If you don't, you might as well lay down and die." His words made me open my eyes and helped me choose life and started me on the path that would ultimately lead me here.

I have the deepest gratitude for my friend Bernelda (deceased). She helped me change my life by sponsoring me in Al-Anon and introducing me to Anishinabe traditional healing ceremonies. Bernelda tirelessly supported, encouraged, and inspired me. She was the first person to tell me I should share my story, and helped me take my first tentative steps towards writing this book.

For her endless support and longstanding friendship, I want to thank Lorraine Courchene. Lorraine is my greatest confidant and is always there for me when I need her.

I am incredibly grateful to Elisabeth Brannigan for helping me write my story. She also helped by listening and supporting me as I was reopening old wounds.

I greatly appreciate Jerry Fontaine for praying and smoking his pipe when Elisabeth and I began working on this book. This was very special to me. I am thankful for all his encouraging words and for helping us find a publisher. Knowing that he cared helped me to go on when I began to doubt it would ever happen.

A special thank you to my children: Errol, Donna, Sharon (deceased), Karen, and Randy. I want you all to know that you gave me tremendous strength to go on in life. You are everything to me.

– DIANE MORRISSEAU

I would like to begin by thanking Diane for entrusting me with the incredible task of writing her story with her. It has been a great honour to be a part of this project. I am constantly amazed and inspired by this formidable woman and am proud to call her my friend.

A big miigwetch to my husband for his love and support while writing this book, and always. His spiritual and very practical guidance helped make it all possible.

Deepest thanks to Darcy, Michelle, and everyone at UBC Press for recognizing the importance and value of Diane's story, for believing in us and supporting us through the publishing process. You have helped make our dreams come true.

– ELISABETH BRANNIGAN

ABOUT THE AUTHORS

DIANE MORRISSEAU is a proud Anishinabe woman from
Sagkeeng First Nation. She is a mother and a grandmother
and is looked up to by many in the community as a respected
Elder, dedicated to helping others. She began her career in
health sciences where she advocated passionately for First
Nations patients. In the early eighties, she returned to school
for diplomas in addictions and social work. During her
employment as a youth worker, she helped formerly homeless,
vulnerable, and at-risk youth who had grown up in the child
welfare system. Diane worked as a counsellor for several
treatment centres until her retirement in 2011. She continues
to be asked to counsel clients, speak at events, facilitate
sharing and healing circles, and participate in traditional
ceremonies. She also continues to work in the field of
domestic violence in an abuse shelter as a counsellor to
First Nations women and their children. For the past thirty-
five years, Diane has dedicated herself to the well-being of
Anishinabe women, children, and men. She resides in
Winnipeg, Manitoba.

ELISABETH BRANNIGAN is a mother and an elementary school teacher. She holds a bachelor of arts in Indigenous studies and a bachelor of education. Elisabeth began her career teaching at Sagkeeng Mino Pimatiziwin Family Treatment Centre (now the Mikaaming Mino Pimatiziwin Healing Lodge) in Sagkeeng First Nation. Inspired by Diane's story of resilience and strength, Elisabeth was determined to help Diane achieve her vision of seeing her story written and published for the world to read. It has been her great honour to work with Diane in telling her story. Elisabeth lives with her husband and children in Toronto, Ontario.

Printed and bound in Canada

Set in Eames, Sero, and Baskerville
by Artegraphica Design Co. Ltd.

Copy editor: Rachel Taylor

Proofreader: Kelly Laycock

Cover designer: JVDW Designs

Cover image: Diane Morrisseau,
photograph by Nik Rave, Rave Photography